'*Coming Home to Autism* offers access you can try out tomorrow – no expensive resources needed! Together Tara and Rhian open up the world of living, loving and supporting children with autism and their families. This is one of those books that you keep going back to; to be inspired, reassured and delighted.'

— *Sophie Walker, Senior Practitioner,*
Mansfield Autism Statewide Service, Victoria, Australia

'This book provides a much-needed practical guide that families and professionals can dip in and out of in order to learn more about development in children with autism. It is full of creative activities and strategies that can be used to support children with autism within their home environment.'

— *Alice Carter, Speech and Language Therapist,*
BSc Speech Sciences, MASL TIP

'An open, honest and positive book describing everyday life for families living with ASD. Full of common-sense, reassuring advice – a real bible for those with newly diagnosed children – and explained with humour and love. It's full of helpful tips and strategies that ALL families would benefit from!'

— *Zoe Garbarz, Inclusion Co-ordinator,*
Our Lady of Lourdes RC Primary School, UK

'A treasure for any parent of a child with ASD. My son Harry was diagnosed with ASD two years ago, and I was left feeling alone and confused. Reading this book has taken me from the isolation so many of us parents feel, to a community of care and understanding. This book is like a much-needed hug at the end of a bad day.'

— *Alli Mac Donnell, Model and Ambassador for Autism Ireland*

COMING HOME TO AUTISM

of related interest

Sometimes Noise is Big
Life with Autism
Angela Coelho
Illustrated by Camille Robertson
ISBN 978 1 78592 373 9
eISBN 978 1 78450 719 0

A Guide to Sometimes Noise is Big for Parents and Educators
Angela Coelho and Lori Seeley
Illustrated by Camille Robertson
ISBN 978 1 78592 374 6
eISBN 978 1 78450 720 6

A Parents' ABC of the Autism Spectrum
Stephen Heydt
ISBN 978 1 78592 164 3
eISBN 978 1 78450 435 9

The Parent's Guide to Occupational Therapy for Autism and Other Special Needs
Practical Strategies for Motor Skills, Sensory Integration, Toilet Training, and More
Cara Koscinski
ISBN 978 1 78592 705 8
eISBN 978 1 78450 258 4

Coming Home to Autism

A Room-by-Room Approach to Supporting
Your Child at Home after ASD Diagnosis

*Tara Leniston
and Rhian Grounds*

Jessica Kingsley *Publishers*
London and Philadelphia

First published in 2018
by Jessica Kingsley Publishers
73 Collier Street
London N1 9BE, UK
and
400 Market Street, Suite 400
Philadelphia, PA 19106, USA

www.jkp.com

Library of Congress Cataloging in Publication Data
Names: Leniston, Tara, author.
Title: Coming home to autism : a room-by-room approach to supporting your
    child at home after ASD diagnosis / Tara Leniston & Rhian Grounds.
Description: London ; Philadelphia : Jessica Kingsley Publishers, 2018. |
    Includes bibliographical references.
Identifiers: LCCN 2017058448 | ISBN 9781785924361 (alk. paper)
Subjects: LCSH: Children with autism spectrum disorders--Home care. | Parents
    of autistic children. | Child rearing.
Classification: LCC HQ773.8 L46 2018 | DDC 649/.154--dc23 LC record available at
    https://lccn.loc.gov/2017058448

British Library Cataloguing in Publication Data
A CIP catalogue record for this book is available from the British Library

ISBN 978 1 78592 436 1
eISBN 978 1 78450 808 1

Printed and bound in Great Britain

This book is for Dylan, inspiring us to make a family home with autism in mind.

CONTENTS

INTRODUCTION

Tara – the mum

Christmas 2011 was the first time I started to notice that Dylan was withdrawing from everyone, including me. His eye contact started to wane and he was no longer responding to his name.

The whole family was visiting and whereas before Dylan had been a smiling babbling baby, loving all the attention my family lavished on him, he now started to scream when anyone touched him and preferred to hide under the table, playing with his cars. At night, he would bounce for hours in his cot, flapping his hands and making sounds.

I first took him to the doctor a few weeks before his second birthday. I was told I was worrying over nothing and that he was a perfectly normal boy and all children developed differently. I went away still knowing something wasn't quite right. I kept a diary of all his traits and started to observe other children in the playground.

As a first-time mother, I wasn't sure what was normal and what wasn't. But it was clear from looking at the other children that Dylan was quite different. I returned to the doctor adamant that he must be going deaf, as he was no longer responding to me at all. The doctor begrudgingly referred me on to the ENT (ear, nose and throat) department. Dylan passed the assessment with flying colours. After the assessment, I was met by a lovely paediatrician who had been observing our session and I was asked to come back a week later for a series of tests and for them to observe Dylan. Over the next few weeks and months Dylan was observed and I was then given the news that he was on the autistic spectrum.

I asked if there was anything I could do; they politely told me 'No, I am afraid not.' They told me there was no cure and they had no idea of what the future would hold for him.

I walked out of there feeling like all the breath in my lungs had gone. I was scared and distraught, my mind flashing to scenes of the film *Rain Man*. Was this what my boy was going to be like? When I got home and put Dylan to bed, I sobbed and sobbed. My heart ached and I wanted it all to be just a bad dream.

The next morning, I woke up with a fire in my belly and my head racing with thoughts. I wanted to know everything there was to know about autism. What would help? What therapies should he do? How would I get support?

One of the first conversations I had was with my sister who offered me much-needed support and cried with me. Her husband was studying diet and nutrition at the time, and suggested I take Dylan off dairy, wheat and gluten. He told me the effects this has on most people's bodies and that it might help Dylan; with this information I started researching some more. I promptly took Dylan off wheat, gluten and dairy, which was difficult as he had many food adversities and his main food staples were bread and milk. I found gluten-free options and switched Dylan from cow's milk to goat's milk. Within two weeks, Dylan's eye contact started to improve and he started responding to his name. I couldn't believe that such a small change could have such a huge effect. Maybe I could not cure autism but I could sure do as much as possible to give Dylan the best possible chance at living a fulfilling and healthy life.

The brain is at its most adaptable from the birth until the age of eight, so I had a few years to do as much as I could to give Dylan the best chance of not only being able to integrate into society but also to enjoy it.

Over the next few weeks a friend put me in touch with her friend who did play therapy with autistic children. She came and did a few sessions with him and referred me to some books to read, giving me games that I could play with Dylan to connect with him. If he didn't want to be in my world, I would go into his.

I found a local play group for children with special needs and began going twice a week. I went on courses and read many medical books on autism and the gut. I got Dylan into a specialist school setting which he attended three days a week. It was intense as it pushed Dylan out of his comfort zone, but offered him a routine in which he thrived. Luckily, with the support of my partner, I was able to stay at home and research and go on these courses that would arm me with the knowledge that I needed to help my child.

I wanted to write this book because I wanted to help parents like me. Hearing the news that your child has autistic spectrum disorder (ASD) may be one of the worst things you will ever hear. The loss of control, the unknown, the what-ifs. There were books I read about ASD with diaries from other parents which offered some comfort but at the same time filled me with fear. There were also conspiracy theory books on why my child had ASD, and books with so much medical information or so full of words I couldn't understand that it sometimes took me months if not a year to get through them.

At the end of the day, I wanted to write a practical book, a book that gives you back some control, some hope that it will be OK.

This is your child. Children on the spectrum are not sick; they do not have a disease. They simply think in a different way from you or me. I am not saying it's easy but I hope that my book will offer some practical advice and support on how to make living at home with ASD easier. I am not a doctor nor an ASD specialist. I am simply a mother with a passion to help my son find his way in this world. To love and be loved. I will never be able to cure Dylan of his ASD, and to be honest I am not sure I would want to, as many of his traits that I love are part of his ASD.

I wanted to include some photos of Dylan, my family, friends and our home. All of the photographs are available to download in full colour from www.jkp.com/catalogue/book/9781785924361.

Rhian – the speech and language therapist

My interest in autistic spectrum disorder (ASD) started when I was very young. I was in secondary school wondering what job would be fulfilling and interesting. I wanted to make a difference. I saw an advert seeking volunteers to support a local family in teaching their young autistic son. I worked with the family for a few years and researched jobs working with ASD. I witnessed the family struggle to understand their child and their never waning desire to support him to communicate his needs and emotions. This led me to speech and language therapy as my career. I started university thinking I would find the one therapy approach that worked for all. I even considered that by the time I graduated there would be conclusive answers to why ASD happened and possible cures developed.

I graduated and began working with children with all kinds of communication delays and disorders, always finding opportunities to work with those with ASD. First a job in clinics, then home-visiting therapy services, next mainstream schools, followed by specialist nurseries for children with a diagnosis or potential diagnosis. I began to get involved in the diagnostic process and became part of the observation and assessment team. I also began to educate parents, teaching staff and other professionals through training programmes. I moved on to discussing services with managers, striving to continually improve experiences for people with ASD and their families.

As I met more young people with ASD, I realised that each communication therapy programme needed to be bespoke and adapted, not only to their individual profile of skills and needs but also adapted through trial and error, based on their response to the therapy. I learned that there is no single approach for all. I also realised the joy of finding a way to communicate with each child and interpreting and shaping their communication. I truly believe that all our approaches should have the primary aim of uncovering joy and providing motivation in learning. I also believe that for this to happen in busy family life this needs to fit into daily life. I only work with children from 9am to 5pm but even in that time I find that approaches need to be embedded in daily routines to be sustainable and effective.

It is important that professionals consider each child holistically, that is, pulling together knowledge of their physical, sensory, communication and thinking skills. This means often seeking advice and input from other professionals, such as psychologists and occupational therapists. It also means not shying away from integrating all that knowledge within therapeutic approaches.

In recent years, I have begun to work with adolescents. I view this as a glorious but often confusing time of firsts: in deep friendships and fall-outs, independence and exploring different kinds of relationships. I know many young people with ASD who are kind and interesting and who are making their way in the world. My professional journey has shifted from the why, the cure, the minimising ASD, to joining the young people and their families to interpret behaviour, social communication and interaction. The aim is to make their next step (tiny or massive) to a happy life. I feel we should acknowledge each step and note the small achievements to give us the motivation to keep going and to offer the opportunity to celebrate with the child.

In order to do this, I feel strongly that there has to be an acceptance of ASD in your life. This doesn't mean not to be sad or angry but rather seeing ASD as part of your life, not looking to get rid of it, but rather to develop a deeper understanding. Your child may not always have the capacity to change their way of thinking but you do. You can adapt the environment and your interactions and create learning opportunities. You cannot adapt without understanding and you cannot understand without accepting.

1

PARENTS' CORNER

Tara – the mum

Having a child with ASD can push your relationships to the point of no return. And, unfortunately, I know too many people who have separated and divorced because of the added pressures that having a child on the spectrum can bring.

We all have the extra worries of financial pressure as more often than not one parent has to stay at home to help their child. We worry, about their future, and our own future. We have guilt and we have blame.

When Dylan was diagnosed with ASD, I took it head on; I took the reins and went with it. I threw myself into books, on courses and fully into Dylan. Andrew struggled to come to terms with Dylan's diagnosis, often saying there was nothing wrong with him and that he was fine. When Dylan would throw a tantrum or be difficult, Andrew would try to discipline him, like any other parent would discipline their child. I was told I was too soft on Dylan and I needed to be harder on him. But how could I? I understood Dylan. I knew what he wanted before he did. He didn't speak but he didn't have to because I was in his world. We understood each other; it was just me and him.

Andrew and I grew apart, often fighting with each other over how to discipline Dylan. I felt the sheer weight of Dylan's life rested on my shoulders, and my shoulders alone. We were so tired from the lack of sleep. I resented Andrew for going to work every day and often told him that he didn't understand what it was like for me.

We stopped listening to each other. We stopped caring. The truth is, I pushed Andrew out.

How could he get into Dylan's world if I didn't let him? I didn't listen to him; I didn't give him time alone with Dylan, because I didn't trust him. I thought only I could help Dylan, which I now see was wrong of me. I was so fixated on Dylan that I forgot that Andrew was there in the background, also suffering. He maybe didn't show it in the same way as I did, and it took him longer to come to terms with the diagnosis, but he was still suffering.

Our health started to deteriorate and our relationship broke down. Our story, sadly, is not uncommon among those who have a child on the spectrum. So many mothers feel alone and unsupported and so many fathers feel pushed out.

The year Andrew and I were apart we spoke very honestly to each other about how we felt, and communicated what we wanted for our family. For our children, for our Dylan. We were Dylan's army and we needed to be together as a family, strong so that we could be prepared for whatever was going to be thrown at us down the road.

The first person I had to look at was myself. I was a shadow of my former self. I no longer took the time to exercise, and I was using sugar as a crutch because of being constantly tired. I had given up all my hobbies. I needed to take time for myself.

Looking after yourself is number one priority because without you, it all falls down. This is my advice to parents in my position. Exercising regularly, even if it's only a short walk around the park by yourself, is important. Take that time for yourself. Arrange date nights with your partner and listen, really listen to them, without judgement. Listen to them like you would your best friend.

Respect that it takes time for each person to come to terms with the diagnosis. Try to find balance. This is going to take time management, goal setting and organisation, and can help take some of the stress away.

Make sure you carve out family time, and time for hobbies, socialising and work. Your life doesn't have to stop just because you have a child with ASD. If you're lucky enough to have family around, talk to them and be honest with them. Reveal to them that you are struggling or that you are tired. Raising a child with ASD is demanding. Ask them to come over for an hour so you can catch up with some sleep. If, like me, you don't get much sleep, that one, single hour will be much needed.

If you don't have family around, there is support out there. Respite care is an essential part of overall support that a family needs. It may be just for a few hours, or a day or longer. Your local health care provider can point you in the right direction.

Deal with your feelings

Guilt, anger, resentment, denial, fear, stress, anxiety, depression and grief can all be part of the emotional journey faced by parents of a child on the spectrum. These feelings are very real; don't try to push them away or pretend they don't exist. Some of these feelings will go; some of them will change over time. Sometimes I feel like I am going crazy; I have all these emotions in one go. Sometimes I think they are gone and then they rear their ugly head again. There is a reason you are having them and, trust me, they will lessen over time.

There are fantastic parents and carers support groups out there that can really help you feel supported and know that you are not alone. Counselling is also hugely beneficial, especially if one (or both) of you is in denial about the diagnosis.

Be easy on yourself, and don't forget to laugh. Laugh at yourself, laugh with your partner, laugh with your children. Go to comedy shows, take yourself out of the bubble for even a few moments and when you go back in you will realise that it's not as bad as it seems.

I am not a counsellor or a relationship expert. I can only talk from my own experience, and in my experience communication is key.

During the year Andrew and I were apart, we became friends again. We talked and not just about Dylan or Luca (our younger son), but about what we wanted. We remembered why we got together in the first place.

I am not saying it's all rosy now; it's challenging every day, but by respecting the other person and keeping lines of communication open we are helping reduce stress not only for each of us, but also for Dylan and the whole family.

Andrew – the dad

The books and literature offered to us when Dylan was diagnosed were confusing and depressing. Here are a few thoughts on a daddy's viewpoint and how to approach the challenge of ASD.

I remember the day Tara called on a cold January afternoon like it was yesterday. I was away on a work trip and I knew Tara was getting Dylan tested for his hearing. We had noticed that he wasn't responding to us in the way that other children his age were. But when she called I could tell from the sound of her voice that something was wrong. All I heard Tara say was 'They think Dylan has autism.' I tried my best to reassure her and told her that I would be on the next plane home. I hung up the phone and everything went into tunnel vision. The world around me was a blur. So many thoughts rushed through my head. 'What will happen to him, will he ever speak, will he be able to go to school/college, will he ever be able to live on his own, will he become violent?' I dived into my smartphone. There was so much varied information. It was mind-boggling and confusing. It became evident very quickly that there would be no quick answers to any of my questions. There was a vast range of possible outcomes to the condition. It was going to be a long and torturous road ahead to establish how Dylan would turn out. The thought of this prolonged period of not knowing how his condition would manifest itself in my son was immensely frustrating,

I felt out of control and frustrated. My method of dealing with this was to convince myself that Dylan's condition wasn't as bad as it was, that perhaps he just had some quirks and he'd grow out of it. We were lucky in that Dylan was diagnosed very young but because of this a lot of the traits hadn't become evident or were evident in a cute, quirky or even funny manner. This played beautifully into the hands of my subconscious method of dealing with the situation – denial. Yes, I knew there were some issues and I wanted to get him the right treatment but I was struggling to see what all the fuss was about.

What happened next was partly circumstance and partly our personalities trying to deal with the situation. Tara, who worked as an actress, dropped everything as she turned her dedication to our son and the quest for diagnosis and understanding the disorder. We were lucky in that we could run the household on my income. This seemed great at the time but would become the cause of many arguments.

As many men do, I buried my head in the sand a little – OK, a lot. I pushed it to the back of my head and thought I was fine. 'I can deal with this.' 'I will be strong and supportive.' I was starting my own business and felt the best thing I could do was work hard and pay the bills.

Tara's dedication became an obsession, which was the best possible thing for our Dylan but it started to have a negative effect on our relationship. Looking back, I can understand all this clearly now. At the time I felt she started to shut me out and didn't involve me. It was clearly easier for her to digest this emotional onslaught of information. I responded by pulling back further from her and Dylan. A year into Dylan's diagnosis, although things were strained, we decided the best thing we could do for Dylan was to give him a sibling. In the long run, this has turned out to be the best thing we could have done. At the time it heaped an immense amount of additional pressure on the two of us and would ultimately lead to our separation. It became a constant argument about whose life was harder, who had had less sleep and who cared more. We were both weighed down with the pressures of Dylan's ASD, a new baby and trying to make ends meet.

Around this time, work pressure had become extreme and Dylan's autistic traits were really starting to manifest. As a two- or three-year-old toddler he had some quirky repetitive behaviours which were often cute. However, a four-year-old son who can't really speak, won't look you in the eye and starts to show autistic tics makes the ASD feel so much more real. My denial of Dylan's ASD was now turning to anger. I would work longer hours, go to the gym five or six days a week and, most notable of all, my drinking was intensifying; I was using it to escape.

My mood was crashing and I was struggling to get any excitement out of life. I was feeling numb. I went to the doctor and explained my situation, the immense pressure I felt and that

I was struggling to be 'present' and feel much enjoyment with life. He prescribed me with antidepressants.

Tara and I were both in survival mode. Eventually something had to give and it was our relationship. I moved out.

I was in a dark place and knew I needed to sort myself out if we were going to try and rebuild our family. I reduced the drinking and got myself a psychotherapist. My two biggest breakthroughs came from diet and meditation and they both had an incredible impact on my ability to handle stress.

The first thing I did for myself was learn to meditate. I never thought I would be able to as I'm a hyperactive person, but I downloaded the Headspace app and it proved me wrong. To put it simply, meditation is the single best thing I believe you can gift your mind. It has made me a calmer, happier and a more present person. Most importantly it taught me gratitude and the power gratitude has to reduce stress and anxiety.

As I got myself back together I had a fresh perspective on life. My resentment of Tara being able to stay at home and look after Dylan subsided. I started to respect what a great mother she was and how lucky I was to have her in my life. How lucky we were to have Dylan in our life. Yes, he had quirks but his condition was not life-threatening. He was still our beautiful child. Tara and I realised we wanted the same thing and that that was the best treatment and support that we could give Dylan: a loving, caring family surrounding him. After nearly a year apart, we were back together as a family.

Nothing is ever perfect so don't get me wrong, it's like two steps forward and one step back with Dylan; there are good days and bad days, but you learn to go with it.

It's been over five years since Dylan's diagnosis and I am only just starting to fully come to terms with this. I'm still not there yet and I wonder if I ever will be. If someone asked where I am in terms of acceptance on a scale of one to ten, I'm still at nine. It takes time, so you're just going to have to take it easy on yourself; don't force it and have faith, it does come eventually.

Early bonding, eye contact and connecting

I really struggled to connect with Dylan as he would just stare into space and was often completely unresponsive. The only person who seemed to get any response from him was Tara and this was pretty deflating at the time. My struggle to connect was made harder by Tara's over-protection. She had him wrapped in 'bubble wrap' and didn't trust me to be alone with him in case he had a meltdown, he ran off (which he often did) or some harm came to him. As a dad, it's sometimes hard but don't accept the back-seat role; a child's Daddy time is so important to their development. You dream of going to the park with your son and kicking a football around, riding a scooter or a bike and in my time of self-pity I felt utterly robbed of these experiences. However, as I learned to accept Dylan's ASD I found ways we could spend time together that helped us to connect. Here are some of those breakthroughs:

- *Swimming.* Playing with Dylan in swimming pools was the first real connection I felt to him, something he was enjoying. This started with a small bit of eye contact and, along with the physical contact between us, it felt incredible. It may sound small but it had a monumental impact on our relationship and one of the first real connections I felt with my son. In Dylan's mind swimming is now something he associates with Daddy. This little connection has been a foundation in building my relationship with Dylan. This has now developed into the ability to have some adventures together. Experiencing enthusiasm and excitement with Dylan is extremely rewarding.

- *Cinema*. At first this was a disaster but eventually it became something we would do together. One of Dylan's first words when he was about four was 'Big TV' which he would repeat. I can't tell you how happy it made me feel when he would say 'Big TV' and I would immediately look for the next autistic screening in the local cinema.

- *Building a fort and soft play*. Dylan has always loved pressure on his body, so burrowing and jumping in soft materials is always desirable. Either of these is a sure hit to spend some bonding time. This can mean getting all the cushions from all the chairs in the living room and throwing in a few duvets. Then Dylan stands inside this makeshift cushion fort and I knock it down on top of him. This equals guaranteed delight.

- *Throwing stones*. One activity he has always loved is going to the beach and throwing stones into the sea and playing the 'wave game'. The excitement of the waves chasing him stimulates and engages him. It sounds simple but, to this day, throwing stones with Dylan on the beach is a special time for me. I guess being by the ocean calms Daddy also.

- *Fun parks and trampolining*. From an early age, Dylan has been fearless and the sensation of fun parks is guaranteed fun for him due to his sensory needs. The haunted house and the rollercoaster that splashes through water are his favourites. He gets so excited. The trampolines help to regulate him should he become over-sensitised. This activity obviously isn't cheap and the reason I've put it last is that unfortunately I can't take Dylan to a fun park every weekend. However, with his disability card, I do get in for free, which is a bonus (for the big kid in me).

Discipline and control

OK, let's deal with the elephant in the room. This is one of the hardest balances to find with an ASD child and is often a cause for disagreement between Tara and myself. Our family dynamic is one of a growing boy who has ASD and a mummy who is extremely protective of her boy. Tara's view in turn is that Daddy is a little hard on him, given his ASD. This dynamic is largely healthy as both of us appreciate that typical discipline does not work with Dylan most of the time.

When Dylan is having a meltdown, if it's a bad one it can be physical at times and I've had the black eye to prove it. Dylan can also try to hurt himself when he is in one of these moods. One little trick that has worked for me in this situation is rolling him up in a duvet and applying a little pressure on top of him when rolled up. This has a calming effect on him. When Dylan is having a moment, he won't realise he might hurt you so there's little point in telling him to stop. Once he's engaged enough in what has become a game and has calmed a little, I can talk him the rest of the way down as we continue to play this 'duvet squeeze' game.

I'll leave you with the following. If you have a child with ASD they are like no other, no matter what anyone may tell you. You as a daddy will be frustrated but you will find the ways to connect with your child and how to make your lives better. Stay strong as a dad; first and foremost, look after your mental and physical wellbeing. This will give you the extra energy and mental strength you are going to need to navigate the uncharted waters ahead.

Two to three years ago I was at my lowest ebb. Today I am happy and feel like the luckiest man alive. I have embraced Dylan's ASD through the amazing support of Tara. It's not all sunsets and rainbows and there are many frustrating days and challenges ahead but I wouldn't change it for the world.

Rhian – the speech and language therapist

Grief

As a speech and language therapist, I was trained in child development and therapy approaches. I had learning sessions in reflective listening and counselling skills. We were taught to consider the whole family and the child, to work from a holistic therapeutic approach. In practice, my sessions would be largely taken up with listening, providing explanations and offering support through problem solving different scenarios in the family. It was sometimes the case that I, the speech and language therapist, was the most consistent professional in the families' lives. This meant I often became a sounding board for their day-to-day challenges and the emotions that came with them. Initially, I questioned whether this was my role as I was not a counsellor nor a family therapist. However, over the years, my understanding of the role of a speech and language therapist in a family's life has evolved. I have realised that I needed to have a good knowledge about the grief process, to not only understand where families are in their journey but also to be able to support them to be the pivotal people in any therapy or intervention.

Much of our decision making in health now focuses on providing better outcomes by involving families and young people in their care through joint decision making. This promotes self-reflection and independence. Recent research strongly indicates that focusing on skills within families and intervening early are integral to any long-term impact for intervention. One particular study (Pickles *et al.* 2016) has been referred to in the media as 'super-parenting' and is about giving mums and dads the skills to improve their child's communication, interaction and thinking. There were over 100 families involved who had a child with ASD between two and just under five years old. These children were diagnosed with ASD but not any other difficulties. This meant that children with other difficulties such as severe sensory impairment, epilepsy requiring medication and/or who had a non-verbal age equivalent of 12 months or less were excluded from the study. Some families were randomly assigned to a particular intervention that worked with the parent rather than directly with the child. The aim was to enhance the parent interactions so that they were developmentally accurate. The other group were assigned to 'treatment as usual' in three specialist children centres across London, Manchester and Newcastle. The families were assessed prior to treatment and then at follow-up (around six years later). The results showed long-term ASD symptom reduction from early intervention and highlighted the impact of working through parents and carers. There is more information on this study in Chapter 9.

For some, it can be useful to reflect not only on how they are feeling in general but also on how they are feeling in direct relation to their child and their diagnosis of ASD. I will now explore a framework I have found useful, and try to combine this with what families have shared with me over the years. Having a framework to consider these feelings can be very useful for you as well as for me as a therapist. It helps to acknowledge where you are, what capacities you currently have and therefore what can be best changed and gained at this time.

Parents have described the feeling of loss and grief they experience when they are going through or finally get the diagnosis of ASD. The five stages of grief outlined in the Kübler-Ross model were first published in 1969 and remain useful to consider (see Chapter 9 for details of the book). This was first written for people dealing with a terminal diagnosis; since then it has been used by many to consider any loss or great change in life.

I have been part of assessment teams that provide the conclusive diagnosis of ASD. During these sessions families have talked about feelings of relief after diagnosis. They have often known something was wrong. Feelings of shock are equally common; they didn't see their child as the same as those with ASD on TV or in the playgrounds. These initial feelings are often quite brief, before parents go on to report a wide range of different and sometimes conflicting feelings. You may recognise or even have experienced the following, or maybe not; everyone has a different perspective. I have listed some examples in broad categories.

Denial

This can be a protective coping skill as you are faced with facts that challenge the hopes or plans you had for your child and your family. It may be that you seek more assessments or request second opinions. You may deny part of the diagnosis, for example saying 'it's not forever' or deny the impact it will have on your life by brushing over your feelings, saying 'we just have to get on'. Parents have shared that this is the point at which they find it useful to discuss detailed descriptions of what their child does and what their child's areas of strength and need are. Providing this information can help them make the links between the behaviours they see in their child and parts of ASD. Some parents have shared that they need to have some time at this stage to process all this information. They do not want to sign up for courses immediately.

Anger

This can result in refusing a diagnosis as you feel out of control. Anger may be directed at those closest to you or to people trying to help your child. You may notice that the smaller day-to-day challenges are resulting in you having more explosive reactions. Parents have explained to me that they want to be allowed to feel angry, while also having some support to be able to channel this anger productively. One parent described how during her anger stage she would stay up alongside her child who was not sleeping and make every visual timetable and prompt sheet she could think of. She would then angrily demand her family and school follow these. She also took up attending the gym again and really pushing her anger through workouts.

Bargaining

This can be when you have decided to make decisions while trying to juggle the other demands in your life. Parents have said this is the time they really seek information on what is out there. They have often asked me for direction on what avenues of support and therapy are available to offer their child. Parents have also shared that this is when they will sometimes bargain their family life balance to focus completely on ASD. The hope is that this sacrifice will affect the change, whether this be minimising how autistic their child is or making him or her more like others. They often explore approaches that promise a cure 'if you have 30 hours with this therapy' or 'if you build a special blank therapy room' or 'try taking these alternative medicines'. Sometimes in the bargain equation the thing that tips the balance is the need to take control of the ASD. Tara herself describes how she went through this, seeking different approaches for a long time. She often felt hopeful, but on occasion full of despair. Parents are entitled to explore these avenues. I would, however, always encourage you all to review the acknowledged research for interventions. I consider the National Autistic Society to provide some of the best non-biased descriptions of interventions. Research Autism is also excellent for highlighting approaches that have good evidence. They also draw attention to those that have a proven harmful or negative impact. You can find reference to these in Chapter 9 of this book.

Depression and sadness

This can be the stage when you feel consumed by it all. You may feel completely wiped out and find yourself unmotivated thinking 'nothing I do makes it better'. You cry lots and take yourself away from school or family activity. Parents have told me that knowing and talking to other people going through a diagnosis is supportive at this stage. It can be empowering to be part of a group or community who share a common goal, whether that is supporting your ASD child to make their way in the world or sharing your feelings linked to the diagnosis. However, the support is only positive if people do actually share the same goal as you. You can have different views around ASD but not different goals. I had the experience of supporting a group that did not work because a couple of parents came with the goal of finding out about ASD to see if this was indeed the right diagnosis for their children. They listened to other members' stories, only to compare to their child and spot the differences that might suggest that their child needed a different diagnosis. Other members of the group wanted to move from the theory of what ASD is to practical advice on supporting their children. The time was spent expressing frustrations with each other and all reported that they were not finding the experience positive. In the end we separated the groups, to allow each to work through their different goals. So, if one group doesn't work for you, don't be afraid to try another.

You may also feel guilt at this stage as you may want to distance yourself from ASD for a time. Some parents have needed to take time away, doing something for themselves or just having a duvet day. The most difficult thing reported was finding or taking the step of asking others to take over for a short time. This can be a very hard stage to experience but it is a useful path in grieving, as you are, without knowing it, starting to face the future head on. I have known many parents seek counselling at this point. I would encourage you to visit your GP and seek a referral to your local counselling services if you feel you need help to manage these feelings.

Acceptance

By this time feelings are less intense and not all consuming. Some people describe a sense of balance, with room for other things in day-to-day life – a sense of moving forward. Parents say this is the stage that they start making planned adjustments to their routines and homes. These adjustments are not always related to a specific therapy approach. It is not giving up. Nor is it accepting that this is the stage of development your child will be at for evermore. It is to allow for the ASD. I find that at this time encouragement and affirmation of changes can often be the most powerful support.

Other feelings of fear, panic, embarrassment and hope are also felt. These are all completely normal. Although hard to experience, understanding them can help you to use these feelings in a positive way.

There is no fixed time to spend in one stage or emotion nor is there necessarily a clear progression through the stages. In fact, you may move back and then forward. You may also re-enter the cycle at different times in your child's life. It becomes a challenge or difficulty if you stay stuck in one stage or if you simply continue to move around the grief cycle without moving towards acceptance.

But what actually leads people to acceptance? I feel one of the most important ways is through understanding ASD. To understand what this really means for your child. Developing this empathy is powerful. It will help move you towards acceptance and consequently being able to adapt your day-to-day lives to support your ASD child.

Understanding your child and your child in the context of ASD can be helpful. I think this understanding is essential to help you directly link why your child may communicate and behave the way they do. ASD is a lifelong disability that impacts on certain aspects of development. Your child may well be impacted in one of these areas more than the others. There will be differences in how your child experiences the world around them, interacts and communicates with others.

Understanding communication development

I talk about communication rather than speech or language because I want you to think beyond just words. Communication development in a child is first about what they take in and then what they give out. It starts with looking and paying attention to sounds and sights. This builds to hearing sounds and then processing the meaning behind these, while starting to understand non-verbal communication such as facial expressions and tone of voice, all of which happens in the very early months.

There is no conclusive known cause of ASD. There is, however, increasing understanding of the brain and developing theories suggesting that there is reduced social competence in babies who are vulnerable to social communication disorders.

All babies look to people's faces and in particular their eyes. After two months neurotypically developing babies start to look even more towards people's eyes as they are rewarded with a cocktail of chemicals and hormones released from the part of the brain called the limbic system. In contrast, babies with social communication vulnerabilities look less, having fewer rewards with social interaction from very early on. This also means that they are less likely to pick up on what is communicated by a look. Think about a parent peering over a cot and smiling at a baby, then shifting their gaze to look over to the bottle on the table. The baby looking at the parent's eyes will have followed the look to the bottle, anticipating that it's time for food, whereas the child with vulnerabilities has missed the looking and therefore does not, or is slower to, predict what may happen next. Studies have also shown that brains of those with vulnerabilities focus more on objects rather than social stimuli. Additionally, their brains process sounds without linking them with the social part of the brain, making the link of talking with social intention more ambiguous. This suggests that the brain architecture is changed early, negatively impacting on social communication and interactions.

Social competence grows alongside the understanding of words and sentences. These words and sentences are mapped onto experiences and often play, leading to ideas and thoughts to share. The child first starts using non-verbal communication, such as pointing or a change in facial expression to share these ideas. They then choose the right words, eventually putting these into sentences. Finally, they will begin to work out how to say all the sounds within words and sentences, correcting any errors that you may hear with younger children, for example, correctly saying 'cat' instead of 'tat'. A speech and language therapist will often refer to the pyramid of communication development or talk you through the communication chain. This is used to help you work out where the breakdown is and what you are going to start working on.

I often get asked: will my child talk? I genuinely never know the answer to this question. Certainly, there is evidence to suggest it is less likely the older a child gets. And less likely if shared attention is not first developed. That's why your speech and language therapist will always want to take you back to the communication skills beyond just the words and the way your child says the words.

Communication as a process

Communication is a process of sending a message from one person to another person. This process can be impacted on by the relationship with and feedback from the other person. Thinking about this can help to highlight the role not only of the child but also the person they are communicating with, making communication a shared responsibility.

Shared responsibility for communication

It is useful to think of the means, reasons and opportunity framework for effective communication (Money and Thurman 1994). This explains that someone needs the how, which is the means of communication (gesture, sign, words). They need the whys, which are the reasons (to protest, request things, comment, make social greetings). And they need the specifics, the who and the where, which are the opportunities created (through shared interests and moments).

I feel it is important to view *all* behaviours as a communication, whether that is of a need, want or emotional state. It is the challenge of people around the ASD child to interpret the behaviour and respond so as to shape this into a clearer communication system. You will often have an innate understanding of what your child is trying to communicate; however, in order for this to be useful in the wider world you have to share this knowledge as well as provide a useful guide for others.

An empowering activity to do with the team working with your child is to develop a personal passport. In this you can share information. This can be information linked to diagnosis, important people and important things to your child: a way to help others understand your child's ASD. An example follows.

My personal passport

How I communicate
I communicate using my body and sounds. I do not understand that you may not know what these sounds/body movements mean. I am starting to learn how to give a picture to you for things I really want. This is called the Picture Exchange Communication System. I need adults to help me use this as I am still learning.

I like…
I like toys with music and lights. I will show this by moving towards the toys, making a low humming sound. I like going to the park and being on the swing and roundabout. I will sometimes hit the swing or roundabout when I mean 'more please'.

I don't like…
I don't like rough woolly textures, people crowding me, people touching me when I am not prepared for it or waiting for things. I will show this by humming in a higher pitch and rocking on my heels. Sometimes I will push away things I don't like.

My sensory world
I experience the world around me differently. I seek some things more than others. I am under-stimulated for my vision and hearing. This means I seek more lights and more sounds. I avoid some things, especially touch. Sometimes I bump into things and walk over toys. This may be because I don't understand my body in the space around me, or that I focus on the thing I want across the room and I don't see

the things close to me. I can focus on details and not see the big picture.

You can help me by...
You can help me by having music and light toys to tempt me to communicate. Using simple language and showing me objects when offering me a choice. Giving me lots more time to listen and then plan what I am going to say/do. Interpret and label some of my behaviours, for example, when I bang, you say 'more' and then quickly give me more!

Please don't...
Please don't tickle me or expect me to 'high five' or shake hands. Try to get me to dress up. I can only wear my own clothes. Talk lots and lots – it's all white noise to me.

This example is for a child who doesn't have words yet; however, I recommend this sharing of information even for those children who can talk fluently, so as to help others understand the impact of ASD on them.

There are a number of courses that can help you explore ASD and what it means for your child such as EarlyBird/EarlyBird Plus and Cygnet. You can find links to these in Chapter 9.

I would encourage you to contact your local authority and/or NHS trust to see if they run these courses or adapted versions of these courses in your area. Your local offer is a document that describes what education, health and social care provisions are available in your area to meet a range of Special Educational needs. Your local branch of the National Autistic Society may also provide you with information.

I have learned a great deal about ASD from talking to people who are autistic. I have attended useful and enriching sessions with Ros Blackburn and Robyn Steward to name but a few. There are many other inspiring adults who give talks, often through charities or at conferences. If you feel ready, I would encourage you to attend.

Emotional regulation

Over the years, I have realised the important, indeed the essential, need to support young people develop positive calming techniques. This applies to children who have words and those without them, and allows them to achieve balance in their emotional states. This helps them to be ready for learning.

Shaping

Your child may express their anger or frustration by throwing things or hitting people. You can intervene and shape this into something that continues to be a behavioural response but a more acceptable one. You could shape the throwing of anything to throwing beanbags into a metal container or magnetic darts at a board, or shape the hitting of people to hitting a pillow or boxing bag. Gradually, you will need to look to the early signs of anger so you can prompt or guide your child at this earlier stage to use the alternative behavioural ways to express their anger or frustration. You can also do this for other emotions, providing not only the alternative behaviour but also the words for the child to say if they could. This could mean, for example, shaping 'when I am super-excited I may hit myself' to 'when I am super-excited I can clap lots' or shaping 'when I am worried I scratch or pull my hair' to 'when I am worried I can scribble on a blackboard'. Some parents feel this is silly, especially if their child doesn't seem to pay attention. However, I remember one little girl who had a few words and always seemed angry in her behaviours. We thought at times she was worried rather than angry. We had been modelling 'when I'm worried I can throw balls'. One day about six weeks in, when it was time to finish something, she said 'I'm worried a ball' and we gave her a bag of balls which she began to throw. This was much better than her pushing over the nearest thing or person.

Understanding emotional vocabulary

Start with the basic emotions such as happy, sad, angry and worried. Begin by *matching* exact symbols or photos of faces for these, expressing the emotions while you label them again and again. Bingo emotion boards are a good resource to support this. When your child is able to do this, you can move on to playing *sorting* games with different people and symbols showing these same emotions on their faces and sorting them into piles. If you have success at this, you can move on to matching the emotion to a photo or a video of a social situation. For example, a photo of a child falling over is likely to mean sadness or a photo of getting a present will likely result in being happy. You can also model situations throughout their life. Some of these will be natural, but you may also want to stage a few. For example, when you can't find your car keys you could say 'I feel worried. Where are my keys?' You can even find the emotion symbol to visually reinforce that this is how you feel. Emotion fans or key rings are great resources to support this; you can make these or buy them.

Helping your child understand how these emotions relate to them

Some children have told me they don't feel sad or worried, when in fact they do but do not recognise how these emotions feel. They may have different physiological baselines, for example, lower or higher constant heart rates. This links to how they experience the world differently and can contribute to a constant state of anxiety or passivity. I often imagine how my heart rate, body heat and talking would be if I was sent to a new country without the skills of the language or cultural nuances. If your child has the language, you can explore how these emotions may feel for them at different intensities. You can help them interpret how they look and feel at these times. A very useful tool is the 'Incredible 5-Point Scale'. Please see Chapter 9 for more information.

Helping your child plan what to do when they need to calm down
You have already supported your child by shaping their responses to help them self-soothe or regulate. You can also try relaxation experiments with your child, exploring techniques and making a plan together. This can involve writing a Social Story™ or creating a calm box.

A calm box is a home-made box filled with pictures and suggestions of things your child has found calming throughout the experiments you have trialled. A young person I worked with recently had a calm box filled with:

- an iPod full of his chosen calming music

- pictures of his family and his favourite cartoon character

- written reminders of the physical things to try such as squeezing his muscles and then relaxing them.

Social Stories™ explore the particular social situation including the skill or emotion to be focused on and other people's perspectives. The Social Story™ is written in the young person's voice and is written in a non-judgemental way.

Remember you can also look to teach your child how to seek you, other adults or friends to help soothe themselves. This is called mutual regulation and it may be something like 'I can ask for a squeeze or for you to rock with me.'

I hope that this chapter will have given you some things to reflect on, including how you are feeling about your child's diagnosis at this particular point and what might help you. I hope it will help you to consider your child's communication skills and how you can explain these to other people. Finally, I hope it will help you reflect on how your child might be feeling and how you can help them develop things to do to help themselves, by themselves or with others.

THE BEDROOM

Tara – the mum

One of the things new parents dread the most is the lack of sleep a newborn brings. However, they know that after a few months that baby will fall into a healthy sleeping pattern and all will be forgiven. If your beautiful child is on the spectrum, sleep can be a major issue.

Dylan and Luca's bedroom

A salt lamp

Dylan didn't sleep through the night until he was five. To help him sleep through the night I needed to create a calming space in which he could feel comfortable. A place he wanted to be, after the lights were out and I had gone.

Interior ideas

A lot of children with ASD get over-stimulated easily and have anxieties. So here are some tips on how to make your child's bedroom as relaxing as possible.

Colour can really affect a child's mood. So try soft, muted colours like blues, greys, soft pinks, greens and violet; these can really help calm the senses. Lighting can also be an issue. Instead of having a harsh overhead light on, try lamps with a low wattage. Salt lamps are also fantastic and can be left on all night. They have the extra advantages of being great for touch and also having health benefits. It is claimed that Himalayan salt lamps release negative ions and can improve sleep, increase serotonin in the brain and calm allergy and asthma symptoms.

Big, soft, fluffy pillows and beanbags are great in a little corner of the room where you can read your bedtime stories together. Beanbags can calm the nervous system, so simply sitting on a beanbag chair can alleviate hyperactivity.

It's best to stick to natural furniture, such as wood, because of its warming influence. Try to stay away from metallic or iron furniture as it's cold to touch and can be uninviting.

Use soft rugs on the floor or deep-pile carpet (or ideally both) as this is good for absorbing sounds which will also help with the calming atmosphere of the room. Added to this it's soft to touch and more sensory friendly.

When it comes to pictures, use just a few and make them large with non-glare glass. Calming photos, including natural scenes or of people who love the child, and are in their lives, are also very comforting.

The moment we step into Dylan's bedroom at night I play some very soothing music as an indicator that we are now winding down. This can be anything from waves to very quiet classical music.

A lot of children with ASD like repetition. Dylan used to lie on his tummy and bounce up and down like a seal for hours and hours on end in the middle of the night. I changed his spring mattress for a memory foam mattress, which is great for children as it cups the child's body like a giant hug. It offers support and stops them moving so much during the night. You also can't bounce on it; win win. The first night Dylan slept on his memory foam mattress, he slept straight through the night!

You can also buy sleeping tents for your child to sleep in if they like to be on the floor and like to get into small spaces. These tents can come with a mesh safety panel so children can't get out and hurt themselves in the middle of the night, which gives you a bit more peace of mind.

Weighted blankets are really good for children who have sleep problems. The idea is that the weight provides a gentle, deep pressure touch that can calm a child down. A weighted blanket can be very effective but also expensive. I use a heavy natural feather duvet that works really well for Dylan as he likes to bury down inside it. I top it with a heavy weighted comforter instead of a weighted blanket, and turn down the temperature just a little bit cooler so Dylan doesn't get too hot.

When it comes to the sheets and blankets, try to keep them as soft as possible. Also try to keep them as plain as possible. Block colours or subtle stipes is best. Having your child's favourite cartoon character is wonderful but can also excite them too much before bed.

Routines

Having a routine before bed is crucial for letting your child know it's time to wind down. Keep it the same every night so that your child will know what's expected of them. Keep it simple.

Here is an example routine of what we do every night.

6.30pm: iPads and TV off. The National Sleep Foundation recommends that we turn off all electronic devices an hour before bed.

               bath (see Chapter 5 for our bath rituals).

7pm: upstairs to Dylan's bedroom to put on his pyjamas, turn on the soft music and put on the lamps. Dylan now helps me do this.

7.10pm: we go to our reading corner and I give him a choice of two books to read.

7.30pm: toilet and clean teeth.

7.35pm: climb into bed. This is when we go through what is going to happen the next day. This helps ease the anxieties: 1. bed time; 2. wake up; 3. breakfast; 4 clothes on...and so on and so forth. If your child is non-verbal you can do this using visuals.

7.45pm: Happy Spray (a home-made spray using water and lavender oil that I mist over him to help him have good dreams).

8pm: kisses and bed.

Your routine can be anything that's going to help your child sleep but keep it the same every night.

Clothes

Oh, clothes are such a big issue for us as I imagine it is for many of you. It's almost as bad as the food issues. It's all to do with the sensory issues. The materials, the smell, the colour, it's a minefield trying to find out what children like or don't like.

To start with I only use cotton, and breathable material, as Dylan likes the feeling of cotton. I take off all labels before he even tries on the clothes as if he associates the scratchy label with the clothes he will never wear that garment again. Again, I tend to use block colours, keeping it simple and fuss-free.

The clothes issue tends to get worse when the child gets to about five, six and seven as, like other children, they begin to decide what they like and what they don't like. When Dylan turned five he wouldn't wear a jacket, shoes or jumpers. Great if you live on a beach somewhere hot, but not so great if you live somewhere cold, like us in England. What I started to do was to take Dylan shopping with me so he could have some control over what he was wearing. Shopping, yes, I said shopping. You might not be able to imagine taking your child into a brightly lit, busy shopping mall... No, neither could I. See Chapter 8, 'Out and About', for tips on how to do this successfully and without a major breakdown on both sides.

Rhian – the speech and language therapist

Understanding the link between sleep and cognition is complex but there is growing consensus that good sleep helps us stay healthy, store information (particularly in our memory for sequences) and process memories. This is evidenced by sleep deprivation studies. These showed that sleep-deprived participants mimicked issues of aging such as diabetes and memory loss. Furthermore, a review by Cohen *et al.* (2014) looked at the relationship between sleep and behaviour in ASD. It showed that treating disordered sleep has the potential to improve daytime behaviour and family functioning.

Tara explored a number of things that worked for Dylan who has understanding of language and can express some of his needs verbally. You can still work towards positive sleep routines and skills with children who are yet to understand photos, symbols or words. We do this through 'sleep hygiene' – this simply means taking positive steps or actions to support good sleep.

The sleep environment

Think about the space where you want your child to go to and then stay asleep at. This space needs to be calm. It needs to be as separate as you can make it from spaces for other household activities such as eating, washing or playing. It may sound very straightforward but **is the room or space clearly communicating 'sleep time' for your child?** It's lovely to have car beds and shelves full of toys but for some children this may be too distracting and confusing regarding what is expected of them at this time. Some families I have worked with have actually put a visual sign in the area saying 'sleep' or 'relaxing room' rather than bedroom, thereby communicating what you have to do.

The sensory experience

It has already been mentioned that children with ASD experience the world differently to most. And each child with ASD's different experience is also different. It is not the case that all children with ASD seek more pressure and will therefore respond to weighted blankets, or don't like loud sounds and therefore need complete quiet. You need to know your child's sensory world in order to offer changes that will actually work for them.

There is a lot of information available to you that explores ASD and sensory experiences. Temple Grandin's book, *Emergence: Labeled Autistic* (1986), is a very descriptive account of the distress and indeed relief that her sensory experiences brought her. There are also videos showing children with ASD's perspective on their sensory experience. The National Autistic Society has some great examples and *A is for Autism* is worth a watch. Please see Chapter 9 for where you can find these.

So how do you get to know your child's sensory experiences? You have to become skilled at watching and analysing your child's response to information around them. I often ask parents to become the detective or the scientist, to make a hypothesis and then carry out a time of watchfulness, writing things down to test these hypotheses. A simple ABC approach can help with this detective work. This is writing down the Antecedent (anything that has happened before or simply describing the setting in detail), the Behaviour (what your child does) and the Consequences (what you do or what happens to the child). Some parents I have worked with have kept a diary of ABCs over a period of two to three weeks, even staging some sensory exposures to record (such as having music on loud or heading to the park and trying the different equipment). They have then sat down to analyse the information for any patterns. I have shared some examples from one of the nurseries I worked with to help you on your way:

Dom's antecedents (A), behaviours (B) and consequences (C)

A	B	C
Sitting on the carpet for story time. Children both sides, adult reading story.	Rocking and crashing into children, leaning back on adult.	Children move away. Adult needs to sit behind him to help him focus. Dom getting frustrated.
At snack time, sitting at the table, children on both sides, lots of choice of food.	Rocking on the chair fast, using legs to move chair in and out, banging hands on table.	Laughing and smiling while doing actions. Getting cross with others making noise.

This and some other observations showed that Dom was seeking movement and his own noise. He was under-sensitive to movement and sounds (although only for his own sounds as he reacted negatively to sounds from others because these were unpredictable). The understanding from this analysis can help you then plan for changes to make things better for you and your child.

You may find you need a little more structure to think about your child's sensory world. I have often used the quick sensory questionnaire within *More Than Words* (Sussman 1999) – a book which I refer to again in Chapter 4.

To help further your understanding for now, let's consider the five senses that may be experienced differently by your child. Do keep in mind that some children may be over-sensitive, which is alternatively known as sensory avoiding (meaning they avoid, try to stop or freeze when they have these sensory experiences). Some children may be under-sensitive, which is alternatively known as sensory seeking (meaning they seek out and repeat these sensory experiences). And to complicate things, some children may be a mix of under- and over-sensitive for different senses.

The five senses and your child

Touch
If your child seeks hard touch/pressure – perhaps they run into things or squash themselves behind the sofa – they are likely to be under-sensitive to tactile information. They may benefit from weighted blankets or a number of blankets at bed time. Whereas if your child recoils at touch and finds it hard to have certain textures on the skin, they are likely to be over-sensitive to tactile experiences. You may need to consider the material against the body during sleep.

Sight
If your child likes flicking switches, or watching lights flashing on toys, they are likely to be under-sensitive and seeking more visual stimulation. Lava-lamps and bright clocks may help at bed time. Whereas the child who cowers away from bright supermarket lights may be over-sensitive, seeking less visual stimuli. Consider having dimmer switches in the bedroom.

Smell
Does your child smell each food and then reject some? Or have you noticed they pull back from people smelling of distinct perfume? They are likely to be over-sensitive to smell and would not welcome additional smells at bed time. Or does your child seek to smell their nappy? Or get excited by strong smells? They are seeking and under-sensitive to smell. They may benefit from incense and lavender smells for bed time.

Taste

The child that licks and eats everything, seeking oral stimulation, may also have under-stimulated sense of taste. Explore strong, sour-tasting foods such as Marmite and limes before bed. Whereas the child that seeks bland food to eat may be over-sensitive and simply need water before bed.

Hearing

Your child may love loud sounds and shouting, being under-sensitive to auditory information. A constant white noise could be helpful for some of these children. Alternatively, your child may cover their ears and shy away from hand dryers, being over-sensitive to sound, seeking as much quiet at bed time as possible.

When considering your child's sensory experiences, do also look to their balance and awareness of self in space, as children can often be clumsy or not consider themselves in their environment very well.

If you have noticed lots of differences in the way your child experiences sensory information and it is impacting on their ability to do everyday things, I would encourage you to seek an assessment of your child's sensory profile through an occupational therapist. They can then advise you and others working with your child about day-to-day things to incorporate into routines. This is sometimes referred to as a sensory diet or a sensory lifestyle. This aims to help your child's focus, level of attention and balance of senses, meaning they can cope better day to day. In my experience, understanding your child's sensory world and making plans for this is very important. It often has a big impact on their readiness to learn the skills needed for communication, activities of daily living and academia.

Sensory integration therapy is a more specific approach to stimulate and challenge a child's senses, usually in a specially adapted room with an occupational therapist. According to Research Autism, the evidence available for this therapy is preliminary and there is not enough large-scale, robust research to generalise the findings. (You can find more on this at www.researchautism.net/interventions/28/sensory-integrative-therapy-and-autism.) Therefore, it is not a therapy approach widely available at this time.

Understanding the bedtime routine

I have talked briefly about how you communicate that the bedroom space is for sleeping. Tara has also talked about the importance of having a bedtime routine for her and Dylan. I would like to reinforce the importance of a routine, particularly if your child is yet to understand or use words. It is important to try to keep to your plan as consistently as you can. Do consider what your sleep-inducing activities are. A bath? Music or story time? And/ or dimming the lights? As Tara mentioned, you can use visuals to support these activities. Do also consider that visuals can be more than just symbols and pictures. Think about using objects. We call this use of visuals to support routine as 'objects of reference'. You can make your own. Get a small cloth bag and put this in the bedroom. Fill it with key objects representing parts of the bed time. An example of objects linked to the bedtime routine may be:

- a sponge for bath time

- a small book for story time

- a piece of the sheet/duvet material for getting into bed.

If your child is using some words, think about sleep and the words associated with this that we often assume children understand, for example 'go to sleep', 'wake up', 'relax'. ***Can you teach vocabulary outside of bed time through picture stories or matching picture or posting activities? Can you be mindful and match your words to the routine as you are doing it, giving repeated and meaningful exposure?*** Some parents have shared successes in using a sleepy barometer within the routine. This is used to show their child the expected increase in sleepiness as they progress through their routine, concluding in sleep!

Teaching skills needed for sleep

Decreasing daytime anxiety and repetitive behaviours for very long periods can go some way to improving sleep. ***So how can we use that knowledge in a functional way?*** You can try to decrease anxiety by bringing predictability to your child's day-to-day life by explaining these routines through the timetables already discussed. You can try to decrease repetitive behaviours by teaching them a range of different things to occupy their time. You may need to start with their repetitive interests and expand on these. For example, if they like emptying containers, start teaching filling and then emptying, also start teaching building and crashing. By teaching I mean showing or helping with hand-over-hand guidance. This has the added bonus of improving general attention for tasks, in turn supporting a child's general resilience in trying new and harder things. Improved general attention also supports the foundations for communication.

Often children's highly repetitive behaviours have become a habit and so I want you to know that broadening or changing this will take time. According to some research by Philippa Lally *et al.* (2009), a new habit takes on average 66 days to form. I think it's useful to consider this time frame when trying to change a habit.

Many education settings use the TEACCH principles to work on improving attention and helping children occupy their time in a productive way. This acronym stands for the core principles of Teaching, Expanding, Appreciating and Collaborating and Co-operating in a Holistic way. It is a method that looks to understand ASD and the uniqueness of each person, teaching skills using visuals and structure. I have seen children progress using this approach, developing critical self-occupation skills. That is, they can complete simple set tasks linked to their abilities. This could be colour peg matching or building things, keeping them busy in a varied and positive way.

You can also try to increase children's exercise within the day as this is generally linked to improving sleep. *Can you step up whatever your child's exposure to exercise is?* This might mean visiting the park daily rather than a few times in the week, introducing a trampoline to the home or swimming lessons to the week.

How to fall asleep alone

Bed time is a time of separation and this may cause anxiety. Additionally, your child may not understand how to fall asleep alone. The key is to follow your sleep-inducing activities and gradually fade your presence. This can be done over a planned few weeks with timers, showing your child how long you are going to stay.

How to seek comfort

Your child may well wake up in the night. *Have you decided what is an allowed way for them to seek comfort?* This could be putting on their music or having two cuddle cards to use. Once you have decided this, you will have to teach them how to do these things. This can only really be done through planned practice during bed times and waking for a couple of weeks. You can use visuals and Social Stories™ to support their understanding when possible.

Some parents have shared that planned waking has helped their child's sleep. This is when you record the patterns of your child's waking and, once clear, you wake them up 20 to 30 minutes before they are going to wake naturally. You immediately soothe them back to sleep when they are in this sleepier state.

If you have tried sleep routines and sleep hygiene for a period of time, anywhere between six weeks to three months, and things are still very challenging, I would encourage you to see your GP to explore the sleep issues further and to consider if any onward referrals or medication may be helpful. There is a natural hormone in all our bodies called melatonin that starts the sleepy feeling. Some children with ASD are thought to have less of this and therefore a top-up may be helpful to help your child get to sleep; however, this medication only serves to extend their actual sleep by a short time. This can also take some time to explore and find the right dose. This does not work for everyone, so you will need advice and guidance from your GP or indeed from a paediatrician.

3
THE KITCHEN

Tara – the mum

One of the first signs that Dylan might have ASD that I noticed was his aversion to food. It wasn't the normal child aversions either. It was not being able to have more than one food group on the same plate at the same time. I started to notice he liked some colours of food and not others. It was the textures he didn't like, for example he hated yogurt but liked it when it was frozen. A lot of parents of children with ASD all say the same thing: likes carbs but not anything else, will only eat plain pasta.

It was one area I felt was my biggest weakness as a parent. I know it wasn't my fault but I ended up feeling like a failure. I could disguise 'good' foods as much as I wanted but he would still notice the flecks of green in his spaghetti bolognaise.

ASD often comes with hypersensitivity to textures. I had to remember how food feels in the mouth rather than the flavour. With that in mind, I looked at different ways of presenting the food to Dylan. So instead of cooked carrot we tried raw carrot. You can try chopping or blending foods to smooth out any offending textures. It takes a bit of guesswork, some trial and error for sure, but you will soon figure out what your child prefers.

When it came to dinner time, I started offering Dylan some choices so he could exercise some control over what he was eating. I would show him two pictures and ask him which one he wanted. This method really helped Dylan as he really needed to feel some control over what he would put into his mouth. Hence the reason why he could eat a whole bucket of sand but wouldn't try a pea! I also tried offering him a broad variety of choices within a category that I really wanted him to try. For example, Dylan really wouldn't eat fruit. So I went to the shop and bought every kind of fruit imaginable. I put them into groups and let Dylan choose which one he wanted to try, before he got his reward. He finally chose an apple and a pear and now they are his favourite thing in the world (with the skin off, of course). They are about the only fruit he will eat but, heck, two is better than none.

We also used some behavioural reward systems to try to get Dylan to try some new foods. We drew out a table and put in each heading, Touch, Kiss, Lick and Taste. If he did one of these we would put a tick down under the heading and he would get a sticker. A sticker was motivating for Dylan because he loved stickers. You could use some other form of reward that motivates your child. If he did all four then he would get something he really wanted. It took us a few weeks to build up to this and we had to use pictures to show Dylan what we actually expected of him, but once he got the hang of it, it became routine. We usually tried new food when he was not tired and was a little hungry. Timing is everything when it comes to this. Once he realised that this new food he was trying was not going to kill him and actually tasted pretty good then he was more on board with the process.

We also use the Dinner Winner plate. You can buy this from Amazon, and it's simply a plate with visual markers and outlines for food. There are 12 places to put different pieces of food that goes in a snake-like pattern. Once you reach the end there is a treat for your little one. This was such a huge hit in our family that the boys would eat everything in the little squares just to get the treat at the end.

I think the most important thing to do when trying to get your child to eat is to remain calm. This really took me a long time to understand. I was so worried that Dylan wasn't getting the nutrients he needed that relaxing was not at all easy.

Like a lot of children with ASD Dylan had gut issues. He always seemed to have some discomfort in his tummy and also had diarrhoea. When I first looked into what I could do to help Dylan, diet came up as one of the number one things when I googled Behaviour and Autism, so it seemed the perfect place to start.

We all know that if we eat fresh, good, unprocessed foods we feel better and we can think more clearly; of course it's the same for children. Even more so, I believe, with children who have ASD.

We had to rule out a few medical conditions with Dylan first as he did have a lot of gut issues. I took him to the GP and we did some tests and it came back that he was casein intolerant. So immediately we took him off all dairy products, as well as gluten and wheat. Within a few days I noticed Dylan's eye contact started to improve; he stopped having tummy aches and his stool improved. I supplemented him with a good probiotic to help his immune system and to build up the good bacteria in his gut.

There is a lot of evidence now that suggests that our gut is directly linked to our brain. Previous research has suggested that some children with ASD have abnormal communities of digestive bacteria in their intestines. And some of these studies have associated specific types of gut bacteria with more severe ASD symptoms. The research is still ongoing for the link between the gut flora and the brain, but for me I have always believed a healthy body equals a healthy mind.

I buy a probiotic in a powder form and add it to his juice in the morning. I think that this, along with eliminating dairy, gluten and wheat, really contributed to Dylan's increased concentration and lack of emotional outbursts.

Whether you decide to try gluten-free or not, we all want to make good choices for our children and there are a few good places to start. I am yet to meet a child with ASD or not who does not like pasta. We switched from the classic pasta to the brown rice pasta, and Dylan didn't even flinch when I gave him a bowl of plain brown rice pasta instead of his usual pasta. It was the same shape so it must be the same. I also started looking at some other favourites of his and started to modify them with some healthier alternatives. Most good supermarkets offer a wide range of gluten-free foods now so it's becoming less restrictive.

Now I must stress that I am not a nutritionist or a dietician and I am not saying that changing your child's diet is going to magically make their ASD disappear. Despite a lot of people claiming that diet and supplements can cure ASD, this is not the case. ASD is not a disease and so there is no cure for it. But in the same breath I do get angry when some people in the medical profession state that diet does not help ASD at all. I think this is also untrue. As I have previously mentioned, diet impacts all of us in our everyday lives, so of course supplementing your child's diet with good vitamins and good foods is going to help their brain function. For some it can be quite overwhelmingly positive, as it was for us. And for others it can have a small impact. Either way, for me it gave me back a sense of control, in a situation in which I felt very out of control. I felt that I could put my energy into coming up with clever ways of including foods and making cookies that were healthy and that Dylan would eat. I felt I was doing everything I could to give Dylan the best possible chance to have a clear-thinking brain and that his body was in the best condition I could get it into.

There are two things that I know Dylan will eat regardless of how he is feeling that day or what mood he is in. Magic Mince and

Our Magic Cookies. Now of course there is nothing magic about my cooking but Dylan doesn't know that.

I found that Dylan really liked minced meat and this gave me a few options on dinners for him as I could put it into a lasagne or have mince and rice or mince and brown rice pasta.

If your child likes the texture of mince you could try the recipe below.

Magic Mince

Ingredients
800g (30 oz) organic minced meat
1 700g (25 oz) jar of passata (as Dylan does not like chunks)
2 beef stock cubes (gluten free) or 330ml (12 fl. oz) beef bone broth (available from most health-food shops and some supermarkets)
1 very finely grated courgette
Teaspoon of smoked paprika
Teaspoon of turmeric
Coconut oil

Instructions
1. In a big pan, lightly fry the courgette with a little coconut oil (remove the outer green layer of the courgette if your little one is a master food detective!)
2. Add in the mince and fry until brown.
3. Add in the passata and beef stock and bring to the boil.
4. Turn down to simmer for 20 minutes to an hour. You can add a little water if necessary.

You can add whatever vegetables you like to the mince if your child will tolerate it. So far, I haven't had much luck, as Dylan is a super food detective. The bone broth is very healing for a sensitive gut so even getting a small amount of this into your child can be beneficial. Tumeric also has an anti-inflammatory effect on the body so I try to sneak this into as many meals as possible.

I find breakfast the hardest meal of the day for Dylan. Like most families, we are always in a rush to get out the door to school or to work, and all the convenient options (toast, yogurt, eggs) he won't eat, and the other alternative, sugary cereals, just play havoc on his system and his overall state of mind. So I adapted a recipe I found in Gwyneth Paltrow's book *It's All Good*. It's a simple oatmeal cookie so Dylan thinks it's a treat and I am feeling really quite proud of myself. Dylan absolutely loves them (as do we all) and I feel he is at least getting something a little substantial before he goes off to school.

Our Magic Cookies

Ingredients

2 tablespoons flaxseed and
    linseed ground mix

1 cup whole rolled oats (not
    instant and not steel-
    cut), divided

½ cup white spelt flour

¾ cup whole spelt flour

1½ teaspoons ground
    cinnamon

1 teaspoon baking soda

½ teaspoon fine sea salt

⅓ cup vegetable oil

⅔ cup pure maple syrup

2 teaspoons vanilla extract

1 over-ripe banana or a handful of raisins (optional)

Instructions

1. Preheat your oven to 350°F/180°C/Gas Mark 4. Line baking sheets with parchment paper.
2. Put the ground flaxseed and linseed in a large bowl with ½ cup of the oats and combine this mixture with all the other dry ingredients.
3. Mix together the wet ingredients (and banana if using one) in a small bowl and add to the dry-ingredients bowl. Stir to combine.
4. Drop the mixture using a small cookie scoop or tablespoon onto the baking sheets.
5. Bake for 13–15 minutes or until lightly golden.
6. Transfer to a wire rack to cool.

Rhian – the speech and language therapist

When you have a child who has difficulties with food itself or the process of eating and drinking, meal times can become one of the most emotionally charged routines.

Is food a problem?

During a training session run by a dietician there was an audible gasp when it was explained how little a child needed in each meal to thrive. The advice was to serve the child's own fist size per portion. Parents were reassured they could offer smaller more manageable portions at a time. It was explained that this was less likely to be overwhelming and that there would be a clear sense of completion and success. One parent said 'We can always offer her more if she wants' in response to another's concern about judging whether their child would go hungry. Parents were told that if a child is eating from each food group (protein and dairy, carbohydrates, grains, unsaturated fats and fruit and vegetables) even if these choices were limited, they can continue to grow and have the energy to play and learn. Nevertheless, parents shared that they did not know when or if they should seek help around their child's eating. If you are concerned about your child's eating, I would always encourage you to seek advice from a medical professional. Please consider these points to guide you further in when to seek help. Ask yourself whether your child is:

- not eating from all food groups

- losing or gaining weight in an unusual way

- often tired and could be thought of as not thriving

- coughing and choking while eating

- showing unusual behaviours, for example, eating non-food things such as soil or pencils

- seemingly in pain and having gut problems.

Let's explore the last point further and consider how to work out more about your child's pain. Consider having a body map available in the kitchen. You can point to it when you are feeling ill or in pain to show where your pain is. You can encourage your child to do the same. A pain scale or barometer (0 = not in pain; 7 = ouch; 10 = very sore) can also be used and modelled by you to try to communicate the intensity of this discomfort.

Diets

There is a growing understanding that many people with ASD also suffer from bowel symptoms, causing pain and discomfort. There are also the additional factors linked to the symptoms of ASD such as restricted food interests and sensory issues. These are likely to impact on diet and toileting habits, possibly leading to further gut or bowel difficulties.

Many families I have worked with embark on dietary changes and dietary supplements. Currently, the British medical profession doesn't believe there is evidence that dietary changes can impact on the core features of ASD, that is, social communication and interaction and flexibility of thought. Some parents report that there have been changes to their children's behaviour and consequent ability to take on learning and develop, much like Tara's experience. In the book *George and Sam*, their mother states 'George's version of autism is very different to Sam's and so it is not surprising that they had a very different response to the same treatment'. She goes on to describe how Sam's calmness and ability to focus continues to improve on a casein-, MSG- and gluten-free diet. She has not imposed this same diet on her other son, George, stating that she does not feel he has the same digestive problems and his complex relationship with food would make it nearly impossible.

If you want to try changing your child's diet, do seek advice from a medical professional first. You will need to consider how you are going to fill in any nutritional gaps, pay for it and plan for it. Also, do manage your expectations as there are not guaranteed beneficial effects.

There are many anecdotal reports of the benefits of supplementing your child's diet through adding vitamins and other supplements. However, I do want to add a warning here. There are some studies that have shown that certain supplements are unreliable. Stewart *et al.* (2015) stated that few children with ASD need most of the micronutrients they are commonly given as supplements, which often leads to excess intake. For this reason, I reinforce the need for you to talk to your GP about diet changes. I would also direct you once again to the Research Autism website. This rates interventions from very strong, positive evidence to evidence of harmful effects. This won't tell you whether an approach is suitable or not for your child but should help guide your reading and thinking.

Communication

For those parents who have shared that meal times are times of extreme stress, I would be wary of adding 'communication opportunities' to these routines. Therefore, the next section may not be right for everyone. If food is a largely positive thing, it can offer the perfect communication opportunity that is repetitively visited. First and foremost, you must make sure your child is not hungry and you are not holding food hostage. You can create communication opportunities when you are offering your child snacks, desserts and treats – that is, food beyond their core meals.

Choices

You can teach this with or without words. To help us think about choices, let's first think about what these choices may consist of:

- A food your child likes and a food your child dislikes. This is an easier choice as it is easier to be certain in your preference when the alternative is not at all desirable.

- A food your child likes and a food they are not sure of or seemingly are quite neutral with. This is a slightly more difficult choice.

- A food your child likes and another they like. This is the most difficult choice.

I would recommend you start with a like and a dislike. You can do this with words or without, encouraging pointing and looking at you and the thing they want and then back at you. You may find it useful to have a second person to help your child point at something or reach for it.

I want to take a moment to outline the hierarchy of prompting. I will be talking about least to most levels of prompting.

The hierarchy of prompting

- Environmental prompt – choices around but out of reach.
- Verbal choice offered – for example, 'Do you want cereal or carrot?'
- Visual and verbal choice – presented visually with objects, pictures or symbols, as well as verbally.
- Gesture with partial physical prompt – this means you pushing one choice forward that you know they are likely to prefer.
- Full physical prompts – the second person providing hand-over-hand prompting (gently guiding the child to push their hand to the object or point).

Some professionals prefer to talk about errorless learning (and some interventions also use this terminology) which in essence is most to least prompting (this is when you give the most help, i.e. hand-over-hand prompting, first). I have known both to work. However, with the latter there is more difficulty fading the help in time so that the child does not become dependent on the prompt. I have a preference for least to most prompting – judging whether you increase the level of prompting by pausing for a beat or second, and if your child doesn't respond or carry out the expected action, quickly moving to the next level of prompting, pausing after each prompt to give your child a chance to respond. This is working out the balance between offering enough time for a response but not allowing frustration to set in.

PECS

PECS stands for the Picture Exchange Communication System. This is a system that teaches a child to exchange/give a picture to tell another person what they want and eventually tell a person what they see, smell or hear. This is different from *you* using visuals to support what *you* say in labels and timetables. This is a tool to teach a child first how to communicate with you, then to reinforce the understanding and potential use of spoken words. This means it is an augmentative (supportive) communication system. If young people do not develop words, it can go on to offer an alternative communication system.

There are six stages of PECS. However, I often consider it seven stages as it is also essential to work out what motivates your child, creating a ladder of motivators from very motivating to quite motivating to briefly interested. These stages should be worked through with guidance from a speech and language therapist and ASD worker who is trained in the approach. You need two people to start this system. Families often plan this system with friends and family including siblings in mind. For this system to be effective and long lasting, you need to offer at least 30 opportunities for your child to exchange a picture/symbol throughout the day.

The six stages of PECS

Stage 1 teaches the child how to communicate by exchanging a picture for the thing they want.

Stage 2 is teaching the child to persist in communication, travelling to the PECS book and to people to give the pictures.

Stage 3 teaches them to discriminate between the different pictures.

Stage 4 looks to helping the child build simple sentences.

Stage 5 focuses on teaching them how to use the pictures to answer questions.

Stage 6 extends the communication function from requesting to commenting, teaching them to share what they see, smell or hear.

I have used PECS with many young people. It is a portable and relatively quick system to introduce and use. Some children make swift strides whereas others take a lot longer to link getting what they want with the process of exchanging a picture or symbol. It needs to be used across different settings, including school, with different adults. It should not be confused with other visual supports such as timetables and labelling. The things that motivate your child to communicate need to be regularly reviewed and refreshed. You need to keep up to date with symbols, updating these when your child changes interests and moves through the stages. I would recommend parents and education staff seek training in how to use this system. You can contact your ASD outreach services or speech and language therapy service to support you. Pyramid Educational Consultants offer reduced rates for parents to attend training; for details, see Chapter 9.

Environment

The kitchen is where we often have the most structure and where we have already put controls in place for children. For example, all glasses might be put in one cupboard, utensils and knives kept secure. Therefore, the first thing to consider is: *can you structure and control the kitchen more?*

Access
Consider further restricted access through locks on fridges and food cupboards. This will stop children's unlimited opportunities and, therefore, provide extra chances to work on communication.

Labelling
Have all contents in your cupboard, for example vegetables and plates, labelled with written words and pictures. This will provide structure but also an enhanced visual learning experience for words in clear categories. It will also create further communication opportunities. The labels/pictures could potentially prompt your child to take the label/picture off and give it to you as a way to tell you what they want.

Seating

I have seen picnic meals laid out on the floor and supported seating with cushions. You could try placing your child opposite siblings or you as parents to model eating. Some children may find that too pressurised and so you might find that they prefer sitting facing a blank wall. I have observed parents use the art of distraction, whether this means children sitting with headphones on playing their favourite music or having a scribble book next to them while they eat.

Routine

Parents have often said to me: 'I don't want to support my child's rigid routines.' However, I think there is a balance to be had. We know that people with ASD often seek routines and sameness because of neurological differences. An autistic adult once explained to me that in a world where she was constantly trying to work out things that come naturally to most, routine was a way to control her anxiety and have moments of calm and order. I would therefore think that establishing a routine for meals, when eating can be stressful, would be beneficial. You can do this by considering consistent timing for meals, consistent ways in which the eating area is laid out and doing something the same after each meal.

Clear expectations for success with rewards

Consider plates that are visually divided into sections showing what to eat. Visual charts showing how many of each food group needs to be eaten a day can be useful. Using cutlery and crockery that involve your child's special interest can also help. You might also consider marking achievements in eating with meaningful rewards explained through visuals. Please don't use a preferred food as the reward, as this can sometimes reinforce the preference of that food, thereby narrowing eating habits further. Or alternatively, it may limit the appeal of that food in an already narrow diet.

Presentation of food

I once worked with a child who at the end of the day told his mum that he had eaten an apple at nursery. His mum was over the moon and tried for weeks to get him to eat apples at home. She bought the same kind of apples as they had at the nursery. She tried giving the apple at the same time as it was offered at nursery. However, he still refused. At the end of term, as part of his school report, a picture of him eating his apple at snack time was shared. She was surprised to see the whole apple was being offered, whereas she had been slicing it up. She tried the whole apple that same day and they finally had success. This highlights the need to consider carefully how the food we offer is presented.

Ideas to move forward with food

As you may have already worked out, there is often a sensory element to food fussiness or over-eating. For some, there is the visual importance; they will only eat one colour or can't have food touching. Then there is the possibility of smells being overpowering or surprising. A child may be over- or under-sensitive to textures, only eating smooth consistencies or seeking the crunch in every bite. The child may like a bland or a salty taste. I knew one child who would only eat hot foods and was therefore very aware of the temperature of foods.

This in itself may lead to very limited diets or over-eating for stimulation.

So where to start? Investigate your child's relationship with food by observing their day-to-day experiences. You can keep a diary. You can then establish where your child is at in their relationship with different foods and extend on this.

Once, during a nursery lesson, I saw fruit and vegetables being used during a creative 'make my own fruit portrait' task. One boy, in a moment of non-pressured experimentation, licked a lime and loved it. We used this discovery to build on his exposure to different acidic foods in his diet, adding sharpness to his meals. For example, we made lemon crème fraiche pasta sauce. This began developing his interest in a few different foods.

Making food together

You can make cakes, smoothies and food faces. You can follow visual recipe cards. I remember one boy drank a smoothie after making it with nursery staff. This was his first ever portion of fruit.

Messy food play

This is unpressurised gradual exposure to food. Try squirting syringe competitions, making train tracks in food, filling and emptying dump trucks with different cereals and cookie cutting soft fruits into a galaxy of stars.

Graded expectation

Tara has talked about this through behavioural reward systems. I have often used a face reward chart to further support exploring foods during cooking and eating. To make this, I took a photo of the child's face or of their favoured power character's face (whether this is Thomas the Tank Engine or Chase from Paw Patrol). I then ticked the different parts of the face each time the child smelt a food, put it on their cheeks, kissed it, licked it and finally bit it, rewarding each little success with 'high fives' or things linked to their passions. However, be very aware not to make any food-based task pressurised by rushing the child through these experiences. I have spent a whole cooking experience simply smelling the new food with the child.

Cutlery and manners

Remember that some children may need to explore food through finger feeding for a while, more so if they are working out and seeking the sensory elements of eating. In contrast, some children benefit from using cutlery relatively quickly as they are averse to touching foods. This highlights once again why you need to individually investigate and plan for each child. Some parents have found curved and/or weighted cutlery helpful for children who struggle with fine motor skills. When you are no longer concerned about your child's eating, you have some routine in meals and your child is able to engage in opportunities for choosing, expressing their likes and dislikes, you can start to work on social niceties, such as saying 'please' and 'thank you' and chatting around meal time.

Top tips

- Be calm.

- Get advice and reassurance about the range and quantity of food your child eats.

- If need be, explore supplements or vitamins that can be added through recommendations from your GP and/or dietician.

- Establish a meal-time routine.

- Consider the temperature, taste, texture, smell and look of food. Remember, finger feeding can provide extra feedback before eating or can be too overwhelming.

THE PLAYROOM

Tara – the mum

Any corner of the house can be turned into a fun place to learn and play together. All you need is a few beanbags and a box full of toys and you're ready to go.

Having a designated area in your house for play will help your child know that when you go to that area that is a time for fun and for bonding. ASD children are not great at following our clues. They like to know what is expected of them; it helps them to relax and to feel more in control of the situation.

We have a tent in our house and we fill it full of cushions and a sheepskin rug. We have books in there and a box full of fun toys to play with.

You can buy fun 'teepee' tents from many shops fairly cheaply. Perhaps you could put one up in the corner of the kitchen or in the sitting room and make that your 'playroom'. Have soft rugs to lie on while you play to make the experience a sensory one for your child. In our box of toys, I tend to use non-toxic toys such as wood as opposed to plastic. They have more texture to them and are more sensory friendly. We have some great chewing toys such as the 'Chewbuddy' toy and vibrating pens, which are great if your child is more oral, like Dylan. These are made of non-toxic rubber so you don't have to worry that your child is practically eating it. Projectors that put shapes and lights on the wall are fun for pointing out things that you like and asking children what they like. You can ask them which colour is their favourite, etc.

A playroom can be a designated room in the house, or simply a tent in the corner of another room

You could include wooden blocks for building towers, and of course knocking them over! Having blocks with numbers on the side can help them with the learning side of things also. If you start with putting one block down and saying 'one', then pausing and waiting for your child to communicate with you to put down the next block, it could be they say 'two' or they grunt or they motion to you – it's all communicating in a fun way, that is in a non-pressurised environment. You can also do this when it comes to knocking down the tower. You say 'one, two...' and they say or motion 'three' to you. It's a lot of fun and this can also be played with siblings or friends, taking turns to put a block down. You could use a visual for this also, so for example a little card in red that you could give to your child when it's their turn and then pass to the next person for their turn.

Keeping all their toys organised and compartmentalised will help them from getting too over-stimulated and hyperactive. It might be best to take one toy out at a time, playing with that toy and then putting it back before taking out another toy.

Play-Doh, and filling a bottle with rice and glitter can be fun toys to play with at home also. Dylan loves stones and crystals as he likes the feel of the different textures and the colours of the crystals. We spend hours walking on the beach collecting his favourite stones and take them home and put them in jars and bowls. I sometimes find him watching TV holding a soft stone and playing with it. I actually find when his hands are busy he is able to concentrate better. For example, at school when he is reading he will always have something in his hands from his 'fidget bag'. He is not distracted by this toy or pebble though it actually seems to focus his mind. You can make your own fidget bag. It can contain anything that your child is interested in and you can fill it with different things all the time. Be sure to bring the fidget bag when you are going out and about or when you need your child to be occupied in the car or to be calm in what might be an over-stimulating sensory environment.

There are many toys on the market out there that help with learning through fun and play. There are 'Emotion-oes' (like dominoes, but using pictures of emotions) that can help identify what someone might be feeling through their facial expressions. There are massage balls for deep pressure massage, fit balls that are great for core strength; the list is endless. Sensory Direct (see Chapter 9) has a great range of toys, along with weighted blankets and everything else you can think of which is sensory based.

Balance pods are good for helping with balance, and fidget toys are good for keeping children distracted while someone else takes a turn to play with a toy. Gross motor skills can be helped with a multi-coloured parachute. This is a fun game to play with all the family as you take turns running through it or spinning it up in the air while the children lie down as it falls on top of them.

It's important to practise turn taking as soon as possible as this is an important life skill. Children with ASD find it difficult to transition from one activity to another; they may find it difficult to wait or to know when their turn is over and it's someone else's turn. An effective solution to help with transitions is the use of a visual timer. The visual timers help teach the concept of time and give the child an understanding that every activity has a set amount of time. There are many different options out there, from a digital clock with a countdown or (my favourite) a traditional sand timer.

The list of suggestions really is endless but Rhian and I have tried to help by sharing our top ten toy ideas.

Tara and Rhian's top ten toys

1. A trampoline (garden or indoor size).

2. Balls: a big gym ball, to hold your child and bounce on, pull them over it to touch the floor, roll it all over their bodies; a beach ball, easy to catch if it's not too full of air; a sound/light ball, to roll back and forth to each other.

3. A sensory box with a sensory tray containing: watering cans, water, paints, glitter, pasta, rice, flour, squirty toys, little pots full of smelly things like pickles or cinnamon and toys to chew on. Dylan has a Minecraft chewy necklace.

4. A cause-and-effect box full of: bubbles, party poppers, balloons, air rockets, gel timers, rain sticks and scarf (for peekaboo).

5. Push-button toys: cars you press on top to go or toys you press to have music start or characters jump out of things.

6. Bricks: wooden blocks, Duplo or Lego (depending on your child's age).

7. Musical instruments: bongos, shakers, tambourines and whistles.

8. Turn-taking games: Pop-Up Pirate, ELC Honey Bee Tree Game, bricks in a tube (posting bricks into a long toilet-roll tube and then taking this tube carefully off to reveal the stack).

9. Transport toys with a road map and things to pass and make stories about.

10. Small world dolls and some furniture.

Rhian – the speech and language therapist

Why play?

Children can learn so much through play. Play is important to practise things we need for later life, whether it is organising and categorising the stuffed toys or whether it is role-playing cooking. Play enables children to map language onto their actions, expanding their vocabulary and concept knowledge, for example, learning the names of fruits and vegetables and experimenting with the idea of empty and full while playing with saucepans. Play also gives a platform to develop fun and meaningful interactions with both adults and other children.

Play is more than play; it is the tool used to teach learning, communication and development in the early years. It takes different forms in different cultures. I worked in Kenya for a time where I noticed parents focused on teaching their children through reading, music and stories, and play was not viewed as an equal teaching tool. However, I still saw play everywhere: children playing with their siblings or in little huddles in the villages, imitating working the fields or playing complex chase and tag games.

The different types of play

Take a moment to think back to your childhood and what your preferred play was. Was it the physical play in the park, chase and climbing trees? Was it role-playing with shop tills, and doctor and nurses? Or was it concocting perfumes and potions?

Now take a moment to think about what your child's preferred play is. You may not even recognise what you see your child do as play. It may not match what you have just reflected on regarding your childhood play or it may not match up with what you see in other children. If this is the case, consider this question instead: what does your child do to occupy his time? You still may struggle to answer this and so it would be useful to stage your playroom/ area with toys or items to see if these toys interest your child.

I want to stress that you should consider where your child is at and not where you think they should be. So be careful not to confuse a child's building and crashing as pretend play, over-interpreting what they are doings as building towers and houses. This is so we can place your child at the centre and plan to their strengths, extending on what they can do and are already enjoying, thereby making the whole experience more meaningful and motivating. Take a few days to keep play observations. The following examples may help.

The different types of play

Sensory and exploratory play
Exploring their feet
Putting things in their mouth
Rolling their bodies on different surface
Running sand through their fingers

Physical play
Tickles
Running up and down
Swinging
Jumping
Balancing

Cause-and-effect play
Peekaboo
Push-button toys
Building and crashing

Symbolic play
Pretending a piece of paper is a blanket
Drinking from mini cups
Pretending to eat play food

Pretend play
Sequencing a picnic
Acting out looking after baby

Imaginative play
Making up stories with characters and small world items

Play does develop and grow with children. By five years of age most children can, and prefer to, play imaginatively. By this age they will also start to engage in games with groups of others. These games will have set rules and structures. This does not mean they won't still enjoy sensory or physical elements of play. So don't be surprised to find your child's play falls within a few stages of play. Nevertheless, it is likely they will have a preferred category that dominates their play.

How to extend and develop your child's play and therefore their learning

Tara has already shared different toys that she has given Dylan to play with to serve different purposes. The toys selected can help with gross motor skills or help to support academic skills such as counting. You may recall from Chapter 2, 'The Bedroom', studies showed that extending your child's interests can also help with sleep. Therefore, building on a child's play is, in my opinion, critical. But how to do it? You have already worked out your child's preferred play, so you start there and extend within this category.

For example, if you have worked out that they like cause-and-effect play, try to introduce a wider range of different push-button toys, such as the cars that go when pushed, spinning tops and music-based button toys. You could also look to extend their interest within building and crashing to include bricks, tenpin bowling and balancing games. Next try to introduce an activity or toy from another stage of play. To continue with the example, move on from cause-and-effect play to symbolic play. Extend their interest in building to building with different non-brick materials such as acorns, or pretend an apple is a ball in tenpin bowling.

You now have the toys and ideas, it's time to teach your child new play skills. You can do this by:

- *Planning*: deciding on what you will try, getting the materials you will need and writing down what you will say and do.

- *Staging:* having only the materials needed in your play space.

- *Joining in and copying*: look at what your child is doing with these staged items and then copy their actions, to (we hope) gain some shared attention. This approach is often known as 'intensive interaction' and many schools use it to develop social interactions. Within intensive interaction you continue to copy your child, tuning into their subtle changes in facial expression, body movement, intonation of any sounds they make, as well as copying what they do with the items. You must also have exact replicas of items so as not to turn it into a sharing or turn-taking game with only one item or group of items.

- *Modelling*: repeating a simple new action using sounds or actions that may interest your child.

- *Prompting*: you can do this by taking your child's hand and providing hand-over-hand support to achieve the new modelled action.

I would encourage you to try any new skill or play at least six times in a session and then for short bursts in the week. I often have conversations with parents that start with 'My child just isn't interested.' This may well be the case but offering the opportunity to learn from repetitive rote experiences suits children with ASD. Remember that your child may well have anxieties about the unknown including new toys and new experiences. This could reduce their capacity to learn. Therefore, a non-pressurised and repeated exposure to a set play will reduce their anxiety and consequently increase their ability to take on this new skill.

I want to introduce a few new supports for teaching skills at this point:

1. *Visual work or play plans.* This is for *your child*. You take photos or share symbols identifying the steps in an activity, a little like providing a visual script. If your child is able to read or understand sentences you may extend this to a written play script.

2. *Play plans for adults.* This is for *you* to plan out a play session. For example:
   i.   I will sit on the sofa with Cathryn on my knees facing me, holding her hands.
   ii. I will sing 'Row, Row, Row Your Boat' three times in an exciting voice while bouncing Cathryn up and down.
   iii. On the third time I will pause after 'if you see a crocodile' and look expectantly at Cathryn.
   iv. I will be looking for Cathryn to pull at my hands for me to make the scream, if she doesn't do this I will take her hands and hold them close to my face.
   v.   I will pause again after 'if you see a lion'.
   vi. I will again look for Cathryn to pull my hands for me to scream.

3. *Video modelling.* This was developed to support play and social skills as recording devices became more mobile and it was observed that some children recited whole sections of, for example, Thomas the Tank Engine or Disney films. At this time, the evidence for this as a tool has limited scientific reliability; however, initial studies are promising. I believe the power of this approach lies in using the child's real environment and peers or family in the videos. This makes it personal and promotes generalisation of skills. Also, ideally, it is recorded with a voice-over highlighting

what is good/what can be said. The child can watch it when they are relaxed and it can be rewound and repeated and then rehearsed.

Children with ASD can often only show the newly learned skill in the environment it was taught. This lack of generalisation can be tricky to understand and be sometimes misread as a child choosing to be difficult.

How to develop interactions and communication in play

Tara has mentioned interpreting a grunt in play as taking a turn. This can then lead to interaction within play. It will be helpful to understand how ASD children work through different stages of interaction in their play.

In play, children can:

- Want to play on their own with their own choice of toys or activities. At this stage, a child may ignore you completely and even move themselves and their items away when you try to join them.

- Let you play alongside them. At this stage, a child may let you play close by and even briefly look over to you from time to time. However, they may still take items away from you and get upset by, or ignore, your attempts to take a turn.

- Start to be more aware of you and let you take a turn or even copy you. This is where you are often sharing a play space and even some toys. They may copy an action you make with a toy.

- Invite you to play. They may hand you a toy or say something to you.

- Take on your suggestions and build on them further. For example, they may copy you swishing a bit of material and then drop it or they may copy your suggestion of pretending to play football and go on to suggest a picnic.

Once again, sit back, observe your child playing and write observations on their interactions for a number of days or few weeks. Then review these and make a judgement about where your child is at with interaction in their play. This diary and observation is, as ever, where you start.

An example may help illustrate this:

Your observation showed that your child wants to play on his own as he pushes you away when you try to play.

You therefore start by *including* his interests in what you do. You play with similar toys/items a little distance from him for short periods. You slowly build the length of time at this play and decrease the distance between you and your child.

When he is comfortable with this you start to *imitate* his actions, watching carefully to see if he notices. Once he has, you start to *interpret* any sound or action he makes as purposeful communication with you, even if it blatantly is not. If he pushes a toy off the table and grunts, you copy this and model the phrase 'fall down'.

Only once he has allowed this playing next to him, copying him, and has begun to notice that you are taking turns, do you begin to *intrude* on his play. You could do this by preventing him pushing the items off the table, blocking until he offers some communication attempt. This may be a brief look at you and the toy and then back to you, or a sound or a gesture.

You can find more information on this in the book *More Than Words* (Sussman 1999), a book I have already talked about and highly recommend.

In my experience, focusing on teaching types of play and developing interactions within the same five- to ten-minute play session can be confusing. I recommend separating these out and working on developing 'play' and 'interaction' little and often. You can try to build this into consistent times during your routine. For example: toy play, dinner, bath time, people play.

You can develop your child's joint attention for playing with others through another more structured approach. First, you need to familiarise yourself with Reynell's stages of attention and listening (1978). There are six stages of attention and listening skills identified. These stages largely follow the same years of age.

Stage 1. 0–1 years: Child's attention is fleeting and distractible.

Stage 2. 1–2 years: Attention is single-channelled for an activity of their own choice.

Stage 3. 2–3 years: Attention is single-channelled but the child can accept direction/instruction.

Stage 4. 3–4 years: It continues to be single-channelled but attention can be more easily controlled and the child can listen to verbal prompts.

Stage 5. 4–5 years: Child can listen and do (integrated attention) for short periods.

Stage 6. 5–6 years: Child's integrated attention is further improved for longer periods.

You develop your child's joint attention by teaching them to sit and watch something fun that you make happen, to anticipate that something fun is going to happen, and then to communicate this anticipation with you by looking or saying something. You teach them to also begin to copy a series of actions to make these fun things happen again. You can do this with building car runs or making rocket balloons and supporting your child to watch, wait and then be invited to do. 'Attention Autism' is an intervention by Gina Davies that extends on this. She has developed a model that strongly resonates with my belief to create shared fun and joyful learning opportunities for children with ASD. Please see Chapter 9 for more information on this.

Siblings

It is understandable that you will want your children to play with their friends and their brothers or sisters. However, be mindful if they cannot play with an adult who can adapt and scaffold a little more clearly, it may be even harder to play with children of their own age or younger. So how can you involve their sibling/s?

- By asking other children what they like to play with and then using this to frame an explanation about your child with ASD's play. Saying something like 'All those things you said are different and Ahmed likes to play differently'. Then go on to explain his preferred type of play and suggest that they could play alongside or with them (dependent on your child's level of interactions) for these types of things.

- You can go on to explain further that 'Ahmed is learning to play and we can help him by copying what he does' and then help them to join in with a sliding-in approach. This is as described above: playing close by and copying, slowly getting closer.

- You can include them by asking them to help you make things, for example, getting them to be in the photos or videos you are making to explain play. Or you could use their names and have them play a role in the play scripts you write.

There are other approaches to support play with other children. The Integrated Play Group approach was developed by Wolfberg and Schuler in 1993. This focuses on staging the environment and using peers to teach the play skills. You have a guide (the adult), the novice player (the child who is having difficulty) and more expert players (children who are good at playing). The adult guides the child with ASD to learn from the expert players (their peers), and gradually the adult guides fade out. It is not a directive model as with teaching social skills explicitly and can therefore be more of a challenge for teachers and therapists to take on. However, I have had experience of these groups and how well they can support children with ASD to learn from their peers. This also supports the ever-sought generalisation of skills as it encourages your child to look to and learn from peers in the classroom, not something that always comes easy for the ASD child.

I hope you will now have some ideas to start setting up your playroom/space and filling it with toys and interactions that are meaningful for your child.

THE BATHROOM

Tara – the mum

Many children with ASD have a general developmental delay. What does this mean? It simply means that they learn new skills a little more slowly than others. It doesn't mean they cannot learn a new skill though.

Toilet training

One of the hardest things I found with Dylan was toilet training him. This was a new skill he needed to learn but like most ASD children he had difficulty breaking long-established routines, in this case nappies.

It's common for children with ASD to develop anxiety around toilet training and this can make things that much harder. The first thing to do is wait. Wait until they are ready. All those parenting books you read, where they say your child should be toilet trained by the time they are three? Throw them out. Those rules don't apply to us.

Communication can make it hard for us to know when our child is ready to be toilet trained. I started to look for clues with Dylan: knowing what time of day he had to go for a poo and when he would do the wee dance. He started to get uncomfortable when he had done a poo, so he started just taking off his nappy. This resulted in some unfortunate accidents and some sensory factors that I hadn't taken into consideration. You may or may not be familiar with 'smearing'; if you are not familiar with it, you may want to look out for it.

It was our first holiday away with Dylan and we decided to rent a beautiful villa with some very good friends of ours in Portugal. Upon arrival, the men went out to do a food shop and my friend Margaret and I started unpacking the bags while her daughter and Dylan watched a movie. While I was unpacking in the bedroom I could hear Dylan in the corridor outside. The next thing I heard was my friend gasping and calling to me 'Tara, you might want to come out here.' I could smell what had happened before I got to the bedroom door. There was Dylan standing in the middle of the corridor covered in his own poo. My eyes slowly moved up to the whitewashed walls, smeared with my son's faeces. Every single wall! Needless to say, I quickly picked up Dylan, put him in the bath and got out a big bottle of bleach! Oh, the joy of having a sensory-seeking child.

Dylan and I organising our day with his PECS

If you think your child is ready to be toilet trained, the first thing you need to do is go straight for the underpants. I know it's a scary thought but the pull-up nappy pants are so good nowadays that they soak up any mess just as well as any nappy. Children need to associate accidents with discomfort or the wetness on their skin.

Keeping a simple visual timetable will also help them know what is expected of them. After breakfast, toilet, wash hands, play. Same with lunch or before you go out.

There is a great app called See Me Go Potty. You can create a character-like version of your child and it shows them the steps of going to the potty. This app really helped Dylan. However, please watch your phone or put a waterproof case on any iPad or phone you may have, as my phone took a swim down the loo one day while in between Steps 3 and 4... A flush of the toilet meant my phone went down as well.

Talking of potties, the best advice I received was not to use one. With potties, we are teaching our children to use a potty only to move them to a toilet a few months later. This can become very frustrating for them and can also make them revert back to square one.

Use simple language alongside visuals when asking your child if they need the loo. Don't fuss over accidents; minimise discussing, pleading or fussing as this can sometimes have the unintended result of reinforcing the accident behaviour. Instead, provide a brief reminder that you expect your child to use the toilet next time they need to go. Save the attention for when they do use the toilet.

Reward desired behaviours

When your child uses the toilet, make a fuss over them. Tell them you are so proud of them and reward your child's toileting success with a treat – a treat that is given only if they use the toilet to do their business. Even if it's a tiny tinkle, reward them. Rewards help you communicate with your child that you are happy with them and that also helps communicate your expectations for them.

Also, an important factor in toileting, as with all children, is appropriate clothing. Tracksuit bottoms and elastic waistbands are easy to pull up and down and you can encourage your child to do this alone.

Bath time

Bath time is a wonderful ritual that we do every night. It calms the nervous system and lets the children know it's time to wind down for bed. Having a bath-time visual in the bathroom so your child knows what's coming next is also a good idea, as Dylan used to put up quite a fight getting into the bath even though I knew when he was in there he would love it. The visual is just a little reminder for them to know that their clothes are coming off, they will get wet, they will get dry and then they will put clean clothes back on. It seems like a simple thing to do but it will help reassure them and they will soon love the repetition that a bedtime bath brings.

Our skin is our biggest organ and what we put on it affects the nervous system and in turn our health. A detox bath can strengthen your immune system, promote rest and relaxation, help muscles and nerve function and increase magnesium levels. Magnesium is great for restless legs and for anxiousness. I do a simple bath detox every night. All you need is Epsom salts or magnesium flakes which can be purchased at any health-food store and a few drops of an essential oil. Chamomile and lavender are preferable as both have calming attributes.

For children weighing under 60lbs, use half a cup of magnesium flakes and two drops of lavender oil in a standard bath.

For children weighing 60–100lbs, use one cup of magnesium flakes, and four drops of lavender oil.

For children weighing 100lbs or more, use two cups of magnesium flakes and six drops of lavender oil.

If your child has any skin conditions, do the bath without the essential oil and burn the essential oil in an oil burner instead. Also available are Epsom salts for children that can be gentle on skin prone to eczema.

Dylan gets very restless and as he gets older his muscles seem to cramp up a lot (due to some tiptoe walking). So I find some medical grade magnesium salts from the chemist really help. You can ask your pharmacist for the recommended dose for your child.

Bathroom decor

As with all the rooms in my house, I try to keep the bathroom decor very neutral. Very calming blues or greens work really well and you can always add in a bit of fun by getting some big pictures in frames with some sea animals or boats or landscape photos of the water. These can be a great way to interact with your child in the bath, as you can talk about the different fish or even talk about how the sea is feeling today.

I disconnected our bathroom fan as the background noise would cause low-lying anxiety in Dylan. I also use low-wattage warm bulbs, as traditional bulbs in the bathroom tend to be very bright. We have a lot of sensory friendly squeeze toys and some cause-and-effect toys, such as a whale that squirts out water – this is a firm favourite in our household. Especially when the children squirt it at Mummy's face and I jump!

I love bath time, as it's the one time of day I feel I can really interact with Dylan. We are free of distractions and noise and the water really calms him down, so he is more open to learning new things or just connecting with me.

Rhian – the speech and language therapist

It is important to support the dignity and independence offered by using the toilet and keeping clean. Dignity is recognised internationally as a basic human right. For people with a disability, activities of daily living are often assessed to make decisions as to whether someone can maintain their own health and independence. Therefore, teaching personal care is pivotal to support your children to grow towards independent healthy lives, and to develop their confidence in the different roles they will have to take on.

As Tara mentioned, working towards continence can start later, take longer and can be a struggle for children with ASD. However, it must be a priority for families and educators to develop it.

The Equality Act 2010 outlines that children should not be treated less favourably as a result of their disability. It states that steps should be taken to make sure children are not at a disadvantage as a result of their disability. This does not mean that we have to treat everyone the same, rather we have to provide equal access in the context of them as individuals. Sometimes I believe we miss the learning opportunities to focus on independence because the focus can be entirely on minimising the ASD and working towards typical development.

I still talk to parents who are told that their children cannot attend a nursery as they are unable to support them in nappies due to staffing. This should be challenged. Recently, I spoke to a parent who was working with their child towards using the toilet at school. She was having frequent accidents. Staff said they were unable to put in any additional measures. They offered all the class frequent opportunities to go the toilet throughout the day. But her child often chose not to go. A meeting was held to discuss the steps/adaptations needed. It was suggested that the young girl would at times need the toilet even when she answered 'No' to 'Do you need the toilet?' The question was directed to the class. It was hypothesised that she did not understand that this question was for her and at times she couldn't interpret the feelings in her body as needing a wee. Staff agreed that instead of asking her the question at the same time as the other children, they would give her the instruction 'Please try and go to the toilet.' This simple adjustment reduced her accidents significantly, highlighting that understanding her needs with minimal adaptations meant she did not have to be disadvantaged by her ASD.

Tara has already talked about making a judgement through observing any changes in behaviour to see if your child is ready to start the toileting process. It is important to understand that children also need to have developed an increase in control of their bowel and bladder to be considered ready. The National Autistic Society suggest that a child should be able to wait one to two hours between bladder and/or bowel movements to be considered ready. Some parents have shared that they work out whether their child is at this point by putting extra material or tissue in their child's nappy and then checking it at frequent intervals, until they can estimate how long they can stay dry. It is also important to remember that bowel control comes after bladder control. So even when your child has succeeded in weeing in the toilet there may well be a considerable lag until poos are achieved.

I would also stress that you need to make a judgement as to whether you and your family are ready. Consider what else is going on in your life. Can you commit to the guaranteed accidents and challenges? One mother I worked with felt her child was ready.

However, her older child was due to start secondary school and her parents were coming to stay. She decided to delay toileting for a few months. Another family admitted they couldn't face the battle; with layers of clothes on and off and the increase in washing during winter. So they waited until the summer months, when there would be less clothes overall.

So why can it be later and/or take longer to help a child with ASD use the toilet?

Temple Grandin said 'There are two major causes of toilet training problems in children with ASD. They are either afraid of the toilet or they do not know what they are supposed to do' (see www. autism.com/grandin_FAQ).

You might not see the changes in behaviour talked about that indicate your child needs the toilet. This is because some children with ASD have difficulty interpreting their bowel and bladder movements due to their already mentioned sensory difficulties. They may therefore need support to make the link that a full bladder equals time to wee. Some children with sensory difficulties may also seek the comfort of a full nappy and leaving this sensation is a loss.

Children with ASD may not realise that people around them don't automatically understand that they need the toilet. They may not understand that they need to communicate this to you. This difficulty is referred to as mind-blindness.

Mind-blindness is linked to the theory of mind. It refers to a person's delay or difficulty 'walking in another person's shoes', imagining their thoughts and feelings.

In my experience, many children have anxieties related to so many parts of the toilet process. The understanding of when to go. The unpredictability of accidents. The possibility of getting wee or poo on clothing. The discomfort of the bathroom environment. The discomfort of material or toilet paper on the skin. No wonder for many it would seem easier, cleaner and more predictable to stay in nappies.

Even when you are not ready, you can get ready to start toilet training

If you are not quite ready to lose the nappies, whether that is because of your child's readiness or indeed your family's readiness to start the toileting process, you can still start to get ready. You can plan and prepare. I am sure you will find in time that planning and preparing are essential for being in a position to teach any skill.

Is the bathroom organised to practically support your child to get to the toilet and sink? Consider whether you have the following:

- A set of small steps: for your child to reach the toilet and the sink so as to support washing hands or even reaching the flush.

- Toilet inserts: to support feeling secure on the toilet and prevent that 'I could fall into the toilet' fear.

- Lots and lots of spare clothes in a mobile bag: to be ready for accidents anywhere you go.

- Your child's preferred underwear: to support the transition to pants. You can go shopping or chose these together online.

Tara has mentioned some bathroom decoration tips. Now take a moment to consider adapting the environment further, to take into account your child's possible sensory sensitivities or sensory-seeking behaviour. These considerations could include:

- Replacing any tube or fluorescent lighting and considering dimming light switches: to support any possible sensory needs with regard to brightness.

- Fluffy towels, fabric blinds, bath mats: to absorb the echoes and support any possible sensory needs linked to sound.

- Flooring: to offer something a little more comforting underfoot whether this is soft fluffy mats or the coolness of linoleum.

- Blockers on taps: to stop the temptation of turning water full on, flooding the bathroom or simply engaging in the on and off mechanism. Your child may be more interested than some in the sensory activity of running water.

- Incense or neutralising plugs: to support any possible sensory needs linked to smells, for example liking or avoiding strong smells.

- Different materials for wiping – soft toilet paper and wet wipes: to support any sensory sensitives around touch with some of the most sensitive areas of the body.

- Toilet toys. These are motivating items only to be used when on the toilet. These can be small toys such as a Bendy Man or Pull Putty. I have found toilet toys work best if the toys are special to the toilet and your child does not have experience of them in other places.

Can you introduce a new toilet routine mirroring the one you will be hoping to achieve when your child is ready to go without nappies? This means:

- Changing nappies in the bathroom.

- If possible, promoting the soon-to-be-used toilet by changing nappies standing up next to the toilet.

- Emptying the contents of the nappy into the toilet and flushing.

- Teaching the washing and drying of hands in the bathroom.

Next, have you talked to the family and explored how you are going to approach the process as one united team? Have you talked to others beyond the family involved such as nursery staff, the child minder or other professionals? Do be mindful that health visitors with an interest in additional needs and occupational therapists are good professionals to be involved in this process. They can help guide you on a number of things, including making the decision whether your child is ready or not. It is so important that your family's approach to toileting, once decided upon, is used consistently. This will help your child use their new skill in different settings with different people.

Understanding about the toilet

Interpret and shape

We have already talked about this and will talk about it more in the future. This means observing your child's behaviour – whether this is them stooping behind a sofa or, as Tara put it, doing the wee dance. You need to interpret it for them as a meaningful communication saying 'poo' or 'wee'. Make sure you use the same words and simple sentences to give your child the best chance to learn these from frequent repetition. Try to further support your words and their meaning with an object such as a roll of toilet paper or a symbol of a toilet.

Is your child starting to learn from copying?

If so, try using dolls or their favourite characters to show the toilet or bath-time routine during structured and planned play sessions. You can repeat these over and over. Alternatively, you can offer up role models (brothers, sisters, parents) and encourage your child to watch them using the toilet. There are a number of information leaflets, books and videos you can start reading and watching. I like Do2Learn for visuals and 'wonkidos going potty' to teach toilet skills. The links to these will be in Chapter 9.

Use of visuals

You can break down the steps of the toilet routine into visual step-by-step sequences. Take a moment and think of the steps. How many steps have you come up with? If these are in the double figures then you need to simplify the process. If there are fewer than three steps then you have over-simplified it! Here is an example:

1. Crouching means I need a poo.

2. Go to the toilet.

3. Pull down trousers and pants.

4. Sit on the toilet for at least ten counts.

5. Poo and then wipe your bum.

6. Pull up pants and trousers.

If your child isn't copying

You can still teach the process but you may need to explore teaching through physical prompting and *backward chaining*. This is when you guide your child through steps hand over hand and then fade the amount you then guide them. Let us explore backward chaining for a sequence such as what to do after a wee in the toilet. You would stand next to your child and help by gently putting your hands on top of theirs to:

1. Pull up pants.

2. Pull up trousers.

Then, on the last step, you would guide their hand to the flush and let them complete that last bit independently:

3. Flush.

When your child is succeeding at flushing you start to fade out the amount you are helping your child pull up their trousers. When your child is successful at flushing and pulling up the trousers, you start to fade the amount you are helping them pull up their pants, until finally they are successful at all three steps. Backward chaining is so powerful as it is a technique built on achieving things quickly and thereby reducing possible frustrations. I have found this approach is also beneficial for those chatty children who understand words and visuals for this very reason. I use this to teach activities of daily living rather than to teach play and communication skills. You may remember that in Chapter 3, 'The Kitchen', I mentioned my preference for least to most prompting for those skills.

Use of rewards

Tara has talked about telling Dylan she is proud of him and rewarding even the smallest behaviour. Tangible rewards are even more important as a child with ASD may glean less from social praise and possibly has more anxiety learning about the new and unfamiliar. Rewards have to be meaningful to your child. I knew one child who would work for bells and another who would work only for snacks as rewards. These need to be meaningful and immediate in the first instance; you can gradually increase what has to be done in the toileting process for a reward.

Understanding the process

By this I mean understanding the mechanics of the body and even the mechanics of the toilet. A young boy I worked with refused to poo on the toilet for over a year and would often get constipated. We worked with the family and nursery to consider and make changes to the environment. The young boy could independently carry out all steps within the toilet routine and was able to request when he wanted the toilet, achieving wees successfully. We felt that he was very anxious as he was sensory sensitive and often focused on details. At times, this ability to focus on detail can be a strength and at times a weakness.

> **Focus on detail** can make it difficult to see the whole picture and make appropriate judgements. It can also open up focused interests and skills and be a way to teach a child in a systemised way such as teaching about the body and toilets.

We decided to help him understand the feeling and processes in his body, the success of which included him staying on the toilet for longer and having an impressive vocabulary of the human body. However, he still refused to go to the toilet for poos, needing his nappy. We then decided to explain 'where the poo goes', drawing a drainage system. This proved to be the ticket, as he later explained that he saw the nappy go in the bin and knew the bin men took it away but he didn't know where the poo went in the toilet. We were right to consider he needed detail to understand the world around him!

Telling you when your child needs the toilet

Your child may not link the feeling they have to the need to go to the toilet. You will need to help them by interpreting the behaviour you see, labelling it for them and then guiding them with what they need to do. Initially, this means *not waiting* for them to ask, but rather *telling* them what to do. You can do this spontaneously – that is as you see it. The language you use needs to be simple and concrete. And if you can get into the habit, say it as your child would if they could. For example, 'I need to wee' rather than 'Christopher needs a wee' or 'You need a wee'. This is because many children echo language exactly as a way of learning and you want to give them the right phrase for their voice.

You can go one step further and keep a diary of your child's possible toileting behaviours and times when their nappy is wet or dirty. The diary, along with the knowledge that typically people may need a wee 15–20 minutes after drinking, can help you label 'I need a wee' and take your child to the toilet before you are at the point of rushing after seeing the wee dance or stooping. Therefore, it can be a calmer approach to take.

If your child is yet to use words, you can match your words with an object (toilet roll), photo or symbol. A speech and language therapist can help you understand your child's level of symbolic understanding and therefore what system is best to support them. Objects of reference may be useful; these were discussed in Chapter 2.

If your child can't tell you that they need the toilet, even after some time, can they still be out of nappies? In my experience, if the child has some control over their bowel and bladder as discussed earlier, they can achieve some level of independence in the toileting process through toilet timing, also known as habit training. This is when the child is taken to the toilet at regular and key times during the day. They learn to use the toilet routinely rather than relying on interpreting the sensations that they need to go for a wee or poo. They may still struggle to interpret the feelings of needing to go. They may also struggle to communicate this. But by learning to go to the toilet frequently in their routine, they can keep mostly dry and clean.

The things about toileting that are often hard to talk about

Constipation

Children with ASD are more likely to attend a constipation clinic than children without. This can be linked to restricted diets, reduced drinking and/or gastrointestinal differences. It may also be that as your child is learning to use the toilet their anxieties have increased which can contribute to them holding on and not pooing. The biggest challenge is to recognise if your child is indeed constipated. Information from the NHS states that if your child is pooing less than three times a week, has hard poo (big or small like rabbit droppings) that is difficult for them to pass, they may be constipated.

Smearing

Tara has shared her story of when Dylan went through his smearing phase. This can happen because a child likes the sensation. They are also not aware of the social impact. It may be linked to the fact that they haven't learned to wipe properly. Or it might have happened by accident and they liked the things that happened afterwards, such as having a warm bath or a parent getting all red and jumping up and down! Again, as Tara reassured us, this phase can be worked through.

Hands everywhere

Hands into the nappy then taking them out to smell or lick them. Hands down the toilet and splashing or throwing poo. Again, this can be linked to sensory needs and the reduced social awareness that this is an inappropriate behaviour.

Increased awareness of the genitals

Some children fidget or even expose themselves, playing with their genitals. I have seen children lie down and rub their genitals on different surfaces. Once again, as you may have guessed, this can be linked to the sensory needs and the lack of understanding of appropriate social behaviours.

Washing

Tara explored bath time earlier in the chapter (see under 'Bath time') and many of the techniques talked about, such as learning through copying, visuals and backward chaining can be applied here. So I will only add: give some thought to being flexible. This doesn't mean avoiding washing altogether. If your child doesn't like the sensation of being in water, can you do a stand-up wash with the shower head or can you opt for a flannel wash?

The bathroom can be a room full of challenges but, as Tara shared, it now involves one of her favourite routines of the day – bath time.

Top tips

- Sometimes opt for a stand-up flannel wash if the bath is going to be a battle.

- Be calm when teaching toileting (easier said than done). Your child is likely to have some anxieties about the process. So you need to try to steer a planned, structured and calm approach.

- Be prepared for frequent visits to the toilet and long periods in the bathroom.

- Consider how your child can sit on the toilet to help them poo: knees higher than hips and leaning forward.

- Have fun blowing bubbles on the toilet (the muscles used to blow bubbles are linked to the bowel).

- Introduce positive smearing activities into your day. This can be hand painting or goo making to replace the negative smearing.

- Have sensory toys to hold or to offer to your child as distraction from them touching the poo coming out.

- Teach how to wipe, making sure this is a comfortable sensation for your child.

- Keep interaction/cleaning up minimal if smearing or genital exploration happens.

- Your child may be going through a phase of putting their hands in their pants to smell, lick or fiddle. During this phase, try dressing them in clothes that make it difficult to access bits and bottoms at all times (ties or buckles) but that you can still help them with when they go to the toilet.

- KEEP GOING.

Finally, as parents you are not alone. You can get support from local and national organisations. You can look to professionals. If you are concerned about digestion or the urinary tract please talk to your GP and if need be a paediatrician. If you want guidance with this and other activities of daily living consider in the first instance talking to the health-visiting team and possibly explore a referral to occupational therapy.

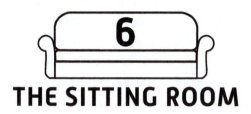

THE SITTING ROOM

Tara – the mum

I really wanted to create a warm, loving home, which was pleasing to the eye. I have always loved interiors and am very house proud, but combining my love for interiors and meeting Dylan's sensory needs was a bit of a challenge. I didn't want a home devoid of pictures and colour just because Dylan had sensory issues and would, more often than not, destroy everything in his path. I did an online course in interior decorating with a focus on sensory issues. I soon found colours that would not only look great on the wall but would actually help Dylan as well.

Our sitting room is a place where we all gather every night to watch a film for 'show time' as we like to call it. It's our wind-down time, our cosy time but the sitting room is also a place where Dylan spends a lot of time when he is home.

Creating a loving, calming family environment is good for all of us, not just Dylan. We have a big sofa filled with big feather-filled cushions, and soft blankets that I throw over the children on dark cold nights. A lot of the time Dylan wants to lie on the floor, so we place all the cushions on the floor with all the blankets and we cuddle together. By cuddle I mean I am usually lying on top of Dylan with all the cushions on top of him, as he loves the deep sensory pressure he gets from it. Much like the weighted blanket at night, this helps him calm down and wind down.

From the outside it may look rather funny, or that I am trying to suffocate him. Don't worry, I never put cushions on his head just from the neck down. He does sometimes like to put a blanket over his head with just his face out so he can watch TV though.

Having soft furnishings is not only practical but is also a necessity for me. I have met many parents who have got rid of all the pictures and side tables and lamps because their child will break them or when they get in a tantrum hurt themselves or others. I don't have a coffee table for this very reason; I have a soft ottoman which doubles as a coffee table once the children have gone to bed. It's great as the boys can't hurt themselves on it, they can jump on it and it looks good. I also took out the glass in the photo frames so that if Dylan did have an outburst and threw them no one would get hurt.

Having a nice thick carpet or soft rugs on the floor of your living room will help soak up some of the sound as well. I have kept all the lighting in our sitting room to soft lamps or lights on the wall rather than the overhead spotlights in the ceiling, as harsh light can make Dylan's sensory issues go into overdrive. The paint in the living room is also a washable paint just in case Dylan decides to be creative. About three years ago we bought our very first house in Wimbledon. I painted the rooms with beautiful calming colours and was feeling quite pleased with myself. I was cooking dinner in the kitchen which was attached to the sitting room but tucked around a corner. I went to check on Dylan after about 15 minutes to give him a countdown to dinner. When I turned the corner my eyes first glanced at Dylan who was covered in purple pen, my eyes swiftly moved to the walls, the sofa and the lovely cream rug that I had purchased a week before. There was purple pen everywhere, big Picasso-style pictures on the walls and sofa. Dylan's face was beaming with joy. He stuttered with his adorable lisp 'Surprise, Mama.' I didn't know whether to cry or laugh. Of course I did the latter; how could I be upset with that little face looking up at me with pride? I soon realised that this was not washable pen (Mummy's first mistake) and when I went to scrub the walls half the paint came off with it.

I love scented candles but a lot of the scented candles are too much for Dylan and his super-sensitive nose so I have had to choose natural soy-based candles in light vanilla or use flowers to combat the smell of my children's smelly feet. Plants such as a peace lily or aloe vera plant can act as a natural filter to get rid of unwanted smells and can filter out toxins in a room.

Putting my children in front of a film every night is my favourite time of day. I have long let go of the guilt of putting my child in front of the TV. I know we have all been told that we should limit the amount of time our children watch TV and spend on their iPad, but I am guessing those people who told us that don't have a child on the spectrum. Now I am not saying that my boys are glued to the TV all day but, my gosh, it is my best friend at times. Just to give myself even 15 minutes to go to the loo, or take a shower or make dinner – it is a lifesaver. I do try to limit the amount of screen time with the boys and we always have a countdown when it's time to turn it off. Now Dylan is a bit older I give him the countdown and it's up to him to turn it off. Which of course he does now as it's part of his routine. An upside of having a child with ASD is that when they have an established routine, even if they don't like it, they tend to stick to it.

Dylan struggles to interact with children in an everyday environment. He finds it a lot more comfortable playing through the iPad. For example, Dylan and his best friend Riyaz will be sitting side by side playing a game together in a virtual world, yet be chatting to each other. It's a world they are both comfortable in and feel in control of but they also love being in each other's company.

Dylan and his best friend Riyaz

He also does this with Luca now he is a little older too and can keep up. Luca just loves to be involved and feel like he is getting his brother's attention and Dylan, who loves company yet doesn't really like to talk to people, feels happy teaching his younger brother how to play. We had a few meltdowns to get there though. Dylan is a big fan of Minecraft and loves creating worlds and building houses. He could do this for hours on end. When Luca wanted to join his world Dylan thought this was great until Luca pressed the wrong button and destroyed his house with one click. You can imagine the meltdown Dylan had and it broke my heart to see him so upset. However, when he calmed down and I said I would build a new world with him he was delighted to show me how to do it. We then showed Luca what to do and we created Luca his own world where Dylan could join him. Dylan finds it hard to talk about anything that he is not interested in, so when we play his games with him and we spend a few minutes talking about the game I then try to bring it back to 'real life'.

We have recently been building a new room for the baby, so I took this opportunity to talk to Dylan about the building work that was about to start and the disruption it would cause to our family life. I spoke to him about how he built a house in his Minecraft world and wouldn't it be cool to build something in real life. I showed him the plans and when the builders started he would go up to check what they were doing. He also started giving his input of what he wanted them to build. We actually did incorporate some of his ideas, such as a secret room in the attic for him to play in. We may have left out a few of the ideas though, such as a slide coming from his bedroom to the kitchen. As fun as that sounds!

Family bonding time watching movies in our sitting room

Films can be a great way of teaching our children about emotions and about different situations. Dylan loves the Pixar film *Inside Out*. It really helped him understand the different emotions and it helped him verbalise how he was feeling. He will say to me now 'Mummy, anger is coming out' and we will try use some of our techniques to calm anger down before he explodes and fire comes out of his head. We tend to watch Disney films on repeat in our house and even I am learning all the words. After we have bath time and pyjamas are on, the boys take it in turns to choose the movie of that night. They both get their beanbags and sit next to each other quietly, for about one minute until the movie starts and they start bouncing around the room.

Luca sings the songs while Dylan covers his ears, and Dylan acts out all the action scenes. This is where having no sharp corners and big feather cushions come in handy. Even if it does sometimes look like someone killed a chicken in there with feathers flying around the room.

We also play a lot of games in our sitting room. As Dylan is getting older, he likes some board games that makes him jump, like Operation, Buckaroo and Pop-Up Pirate. These games are great because playing them teaches him to take turns and he loves the anticipation of waiting for his turn. Dylan also loves Connect 4 because again he loves the taking turns but also likes to count; it is also very simple to follow and it involves matching and patterns. We do have to limit expectations though as Dylan likes to win, and if he doesn't, meltdown can occur. So when we play games I say to Dylan before we start 'It's OK if you don't win this game because it's nice sometimes to let others win.'

One thing I have always tried to do is to have play dates at the house. I find that if Dylan has someone in his house and I can help them play games together and have guided play dates, it helps Dylan's friendships. During our guided play dates, we do things such as play board games together or we go out and do an activity that I know Dylan enjoys. We go to the movies and have a chat about the movie afterwards. By doing fun things together the other children can have fun with Dylan and I can help them understand him and his ways. When he goes to school on Monday he loves talking to the children about what they did on the weekend and they have chats about it. Dylan loves having friends and he is very popular at school. The other children do ask questions like why he wears ear defenders in busy places and I can then explain to them that Dylan has sensitive ears and sometimes the noise is too much. They can try the ear defenders to see what they are like themselves. This creates understanding and Dylan's teacher told me that when he is in class if it gets too loud his friends will say 'It needs to be a bit quieter so Dylan won't get upset.' It's sometimes hard work always having play dates all the time but the benefits outweigh the hassle 100 to 1.

The sitting room is also a place for me so I want it to be beautiful and functional. It's a place at night where I sit even for 20 minutes and read a mind-numbing magazine or watch a film. It's so important to switch off and have some 'me time'. We can be all things to all people and forget ourselves. That's why I surround myself with pretty pictures of my family and have a cosy blanket to throw over myself while enjoying a very medicinal glass of red wine. To be honest I get so over-sensitised myself after a hectic day with the kids that I love the calming atmosphere of the sitting room myself. I have big baskets to throw all the toys in and I hide all the kiddie stuff so in the evening it becomes a grown-up space.

Rhian – the speech and language therapist

Over the years, I have been in many sitting rooms of family homes, all of which have been very different but consistent as the place offered to try out various therapy games. A room for all the family. Mum's big television for movies. Dad's pile of computer magazines. The children's favourite cuddly toys and their various screens. A space, no matter how small, for family togetherness and a sense of somewhere for each member of the family.

Family time

A major challenge to family time in this shared space is all the competing sources of attention. By this I mean the competing sources for each family member, whether this is social media, TV, work and school tasks. Families have shared they have felt lost in this challenge. I have often joined people to seek a solution – to plan for opportunities to be together doing something as a family. This process of thinking and planning for family time can be even more difficult if you have a child with ASD. Your child's competing sources of attention can be broader, more unexpected and more difficult to challenge. These competing sources not only include those already mentioned but also expand to the joy or calmness taken from looking at their own hands or from hearing the click from switching lights on and off.

I would like to share some examples from my time spent with families, in schools and nurseries. These may help you to consider what you can do to create family time.

In many schools the constant dilemma is how to balance teaching with restful time. This has often meant that the pragmatics, that is the social skills and activities, were taught in isolated 'social groups' but rarely presented explicitly throughout the curriculum. The Social Communication Emotional Regulation Transactional Support (SCERTS) framework emphasises that teaching social communication and emotional regulation skills is of equal importance to teaching academic subjects. It is a research-based educational framework that a number of different professionals can work within to address some of the challenges faced by an autistic person.

In one of my schools we trialled embedding the philosophy of this framework through the day. On arrival, the children would have time to recover from the morning routine and travel with controlled 'free' computer games (this means that these were never earned or negotiated on according to behaviour). A countdown visual system was used to support these ending. The young people were then brought together for fun social experiences. These were planned with explicit rules explained by words and pictures. These were for a manageable period of ten minutes before a short 'my choice' was given. Then the children would start the academic day. Similarly, this was repeated at break and lunch time, like a social sandwich: my choice, group time, my choice. Meaning the often challenging social activity was surrounded by easier rewarding tasks. Initially there was reluctance but once this new routine was established, the children began enjoying the activities and linking the feeling good with time with their class members. The selection of activities was key. These needed to be considered in terms of the individual members of the group. For example, one member found any kind of singing upsetting so singing games were avoided. Another member needed to sit facing away and would only turn to face the group when rules were clear and after he had had the experience of watching others have their turn. The group activities needed to be frequent enough to enable familiarity and prediction, but changed often enough to keep interest and motivation. The group activities included:

- *Number games* (numbers were a passionate interest for one group member). One number game involves working as a group to count to 21. It starts with all group members sitting. Then someone stands up saying one, two or three numbers in a sequence before sitting down again. The next person to stand up would follow on from the last number said. The aim is to get to 21 without speaking over each other. The standing and sitting helps signal turn taking more explicitly. This was faded when the children were used to it and they then needed to rely on reading the subtler non-verbal social skills, such as looking at each other to see who might be the one preparing to speak next.

- *Material games.* One favourite material game involves all group members standing close together holding a piece of elasticated material. They then count to ten while stepping backwards until the fabric is taut, finally letting go of the material all at the same time. The person who the material lands on gets to talk for one minute on their chosen subject. All the group members are able to see question cards placed around them to prompt them to ask the person questions about what they talked about.

- *Giant Jenga.* Group members take it in turns to remove a piece and place it on top. Sometimes silly instructions are placed on the Jenga pieces such as 'hoot like an owl' or 'blow kisses to the person next to you'. Sometimes, questions were written for the person to ask a chosen member. For example, 'Ask Jason – what is your favourite colour?'

- *The ball of wool.* All the group stand in a circle. The person holding the wool will call someone's name before throwing the ball to them, unwinding the wool a bit at a time. This is good for learning people's names and how to get their attention. This makes an interesting and funny web.

- *Hand chain.* All group members hold hands and the group chooses a leader. The leader breaks the chain and gently leads the linked people under joined arms or behind group members to make a human knot. This practises touch and giving and following instructions. Once everyone is tangled, the leader tries to retrace their steps to get the knot undone.

You may feel these games are too contrived for family time. However, if you think back to family get-togethers or even meeting with groups of friends you may well recall silly games, card games or board games. These games may be visited less frequently in your lives and at times are extremely complicated to play. However, they get everyone together with a shared experience, sometimes becoming traditions and often remembered fondly.

Family time doesn't always have to involve a game. One family shared how their family time is exploring the day and weather. They use a visual board selecting the day and then what the weather has been like. They had prepared weather experiences. Feeling water from a spray – rain. Feeling air from a fan – wind. Holding hand heat bags – sun. They picked this activity as their boy loved puddles and he was very motivated by sensory experiences. The other younger siblings also loved this activity. They would all sit around in the lounge for ten minutes before everyone would then run off to their toys or iPads. Another family shared that they all watched their little girl's favourite episode of Peppa Pig. They would then all find the items (pre-prepared) from the episode and explore these or even act out the episode together. They would then ask the siblings to choose their favourite programme and they would repeat this activity. This didn't always hold the child with ASD's interest but nonetheless is was important for the siblings to have family focus with value placed on their interests. All these activities have potential for vocabulary and academic learning; however, the main aim is to share a focus for something that is social and fun.

'Me time'

There also needs to be time for you to follow your own interests in a shared space. For the child with ASD, this can mean time to hand flap or to watch repeats on the iPad, look at books around their passions or to simply sit and stare. We all need time to 'download' or indeed shut down for a while. Many parents I know feel very uncomfortable with this; however, autistic adolescents and adults have shared with me that even as they grow, they need time out for sensory repetitive experiences. I knew one 15-year-old who after a day of sitting his exams would come home and switch a favoured lamp on and off while flapping his hands for half an hour before helping out with dinner and doing his homework. As mentioned previously you can help to extend the way in which your children can regulate their emotional highs and lows. You can teach more varied ways to relax and to involve other people, for example, looking to you for a squeeze or for help to distract themselves. Or you can teach them feel-good techniques they can do by themselves such as jumping or getting a blanket to bury under. If you think about it, as adults you have tried and found out that certain things make you feel better. That glass of wine. The long walk or run. The hot bubble bath. Singing and dancing around the kitchen. Your children have also tried some things out and discovered by accident some things that feel good. This may be rocking, flicking their fingers or humming. In Chapter 6 Tara talks about Dylan going to his trampoline for an extended period of calming or his own time. **Can you take an activity that you have noticed your child enjoys (maybe through your play observations) and extend on this?** For example, if you have noticed they enjoy rocking, encourage them to also move rhythmically to some music or join in with some chanting songs.

In school, I recently completed a calming experiment list with the students in a group. We initially focused on understanding some emotion words, matching them to line drawings, photos and events. We then mapped our days and thought about the different feelings we had. We found what made us hot or angry and completed five-point scales. Finally, we explored things that felt good while thinking about all our different senses. If you look at Chapter 2, the bedroom chapter, we explore the sensory elements in more detail. Children practised the feel-good things that worked for them in the group and then out in the class. They rated which were best for them over the week. These were included in their five-point scale and each put items or cue cards for the ones they chose in a calm box.

I want to briefly think about 'me time' in a different way. This is about how to help your child understand who they are and what their name is. This is something we worked on lots within nursery. Parents reported 'He doesn't respond when I call' or 'He doesn't seem to know his name.' Now is this because he doesn't understand that Joe (for example) is his label? Or is it that he is not motivated to respond? You can work on your child understanding their name and responding to you when you call at the same time. You can raise awareness of their name through mirror work: both looking at yourselves in the mirror, while you tickle or brush different parts of their face or body with a feather. Labelling as you do it, for example, 'Joe's nose, Joe's arms'. You can also create a personal book with lots of photos of your child doing things and again label together, for example, 'Joe is jumping'. I am aware this contradicts slightly what I mentioned in Chapter 5 – saying things as your child would if they could. However, this has the explicit purpose of working on their name and is linked to specific tasks. Once your child understands their name you can use these same activities to work on 'me' or 'I'. You can also try a behavioural reward system in which you call their name while you are standing close by, holding a sound-making favourite toy, and they get to play with that toy once they have turned or looked towards you when you call. Be sure to change the motivators as you don't want them to think the light ball is called (for example) Joe! You can consider how to prompt your child to turn to their name and then fade these prompts.

Celebrating and developing focused interests

I believe we should challenge all those people involved in working with autistic children to find and support them to develop passions and interests. Stephen Wiltshire is a talented young artist with a PhD in art. It was noticed that his only interest was drawing and this was used not only to motivate him to communicate but was focused on and developed by teachers and specialists in the world of art. I do not wish to imply that all children and young people have a special talent but I would love to encourage you all to explore what your child's focused interests are to help them occupy their time and develop skills in this chosen area. I remember one young man who loved what most would say was destroying – ripping, crashing and taking things apart. His parents created a corner full of boxes of built Lego, connected pipes and threaded beads. He would enjoy 20–30 minutes going through these and taking them apart. His parents then rebuilt his creations in front of the TV at night. They hoped they could eventually link this in with mechanics and work towards taking apart and putting things together. This leads me to briefly mention an approach called Lego therapy. This evolved exactly because Lego for many was often a special interest, something intrinsically motivating. This was used to then work on social skills such as being flexible in the different roles of the builder, supplier and engineer. This involved learning to take turns, to listen and to ask for help.

Homework/shared learning from school

As you may have gathered, much of what you envisioned as a parent still applies for your child with ASD, although it may be with more consideration and planning. Any parent would be expected to help their child with homework/home-learning tasks.

It may be making that volcano or writing about your family. For your child with ASD, homework to begin with is likely to be more related to teaching day-to-day activities of living or socialising: the things that you don't usually have to explicitly teach other children. However, what we know is that generalisation is more difficult for our children. Therefore, bringing the same learning to different people and places is vital, as is a consistent approach to teaching a skill, like the team approach decided on for toileting. This team approach is championed by whatever therapy or education you read about. Also, we know that due to many children's communication difficulties, talking about their school day to their parents or indeed talking about home to teaching staff can be a challenge.

So how can you help? Use home–school/home–grandparent's communication books. This can be as simple as sharing photos with your child about their day in the different places with different people. You can talk about them using simple sentences, saying it as they would if they could: 'Look, I counted my classmates' or 'Look, I played with Nana in the garden.'

I also want to mention something I discussed with a 15-year-old recently diagnosed. He shared a paper written by Simon Baron-Cohen (see Chapter 9 for details) and his theory about systemising that he wanted to discuss. Systemising is often a skill for people with ASD. This is the drive to analyse or construct a system. It might be a mechanical system (e.g. a machine or a spinning wheel), an abstract system (e.g. number patterns), a natural system (e.g. water flow or the weather), or a collectible system (e.g. classifying objects such as DVDs by author or toy cars by shape, colour or size). I explored with this young boy how we could use this theory to adapt much of how we teach skills related to communication or activities of daily living. We explored using flow charts, scales, stories with clear parts (such as connecting trains) as a system to teach these things. He talked about this theory which shifts the thinking that we need to teach people with ASD to overcome mind-blindness by seeing the whole picture; instead, it suggests teaching them in a system that is already a strength. We also discussed the many critics of this theory. However, we concluded it was a useful one to explore.

Screen time

Overall, I believe that TV/screen time has brought more positive experiences and opportunities than negative ones. In fact, technology is an area that I feel has offered us the biggest strides to raising awareness of and supporting our community with ASD. Tablets and iPads are excellent sources of therapy and education. They provide a sense of self-occupation and productivity and have allowed many people of all ages to reach out to form genuine friendships online. I also know many families who at different points have turned to the web and community groups for invaluable support in their daily lives whether it is around parenting, housing issues or how to cope with aspects of ASD. Technology has brought many young people with ASD successful career opportunities. In our office chapter, you will see some of mine and Tara's top recommendations around apps and online community groups.

However, it is an area that has grown so quickly, particularly in accessibility on multiple types of screen. This fast growth means we are yet to understand possible negative consequences and fully understand how to teach safe and appropriate use of technology. *So what level of screen time can children have to continue with a healthy lifestyle?* I do not believe in providing a prescription for the maximum hours to be exposed, but rather in guiding and informing people on what it is a child needs, any child with or without ASD, for good wellbeing. Public Health

England talks about what it is a child associates with wellbeing and what we know promotes healthy bodies and minds. There is a consistent theme of being active, eating healthy foods and limiting screen time. Also, if children are accessing screen time for long periods, what are they are missing out on? There is no evidence to suggest that screen time can benefit toddlers and babies but lots to suggest it can delay language and literacy and so I would recommend low amounts of TV/video games and no use of iPads for games for children under two years of age.

All children need to be taught how to access and use technology not only to be safe from dangerous situations but also to keep their minds and bodies safe. Over recent years, families have shared their top tips:

- Using timers. In fact, you can simply use the iPad timer and explain 'The iPad will tell you when you need a break' and when the alarm goes off your child can move on and have a break. You can take it a step further and download apps that enable you to set the amount of time you want your child to play and the amount of time the iPad will be locked/inaccessible to your child.

- Keeping all screens out of the bedroom.

- Charging technology in shared spaces after a certain time at nights, to reinforce capping its use especially as you are winding down for bed time.

- Encouraging children to balance screen and non-screen time. One parent had a kitchen scale with weights representing 30 minutes. Each day the child had to weigh out his exercise, playing, talking and screen time weights. The rule was that the screen time could never be heavier than the others.

Some parents have shared 'Well, I don't know anything about this Snapchat so I can't even talk to him about it.' I think you need to learn about online and screen safety and as with any skill such as reading or cooking, you need to spend time doing and talking about it together. You can link in with the basic principles around socialisation in general and these can include the following:

- Talk about tech safety in general from viruses to passwords. When you use programs such as RESPECT, take time to explain them.

- Be present for internet browsing and use.

- As with friendships, advise your child not to talk to strangers, not to accept or expect to give gifts, not to post anything you wouldn't say or do in real life (this last one will need some guidance).

There is a comprehensive guide offered by the National Society for the Prevention of Cruelty to Children (NSPCC) website on online safety (www.nspcc.org.uk/online-safety) and do speak to your schools for further advice. One top tip a parent gave me was that she would simply have a check-in for five minutes each day with her child. They would look at what have they had done online today. She had all access to her child's passwords and they would look at browser history together and talk about any potential dangers. Of course, this is something you may not need to worry about for a few years yet with your child. But you may want to start reading up!

THE GARDEN AND BEYOND

Tara – the mum

Whether you have a small patio garden, a balcony or a big sprawling garden or even just a windowsill, you can make a lovely sensory area for your child. A sensory garden is an environment that is designed with the purpose of stimulating the senses. Children and adults with ASD can sometimes have extreme reactions to sensory stimulation. They can either be stimulated too much or too little. A sensory garden can be very therapeutic and can be used as a calming place and a gentle way to stimulate the senses.

Depending on your child's needs, you can either create a sensory garden primarily focusing on one sense or incorporating them all. The garden should encourage them to interact with the environment around them, to help them with their touch, smell and taste. It should be a place to feel safe and comfortable to explore their senses without feeling overwhelmed by them.

When planning your sensory garden, it's important to feature elements that appeal to all five senses. Visual stimulation, sight and colours are important. You can cluster some brightly coloured flowers together by using energising colours, restful colours and soft colours. Roses naturally release a sweet scent that will attract butterflies and bees. Bird houses and bird baths are also great to have outside as they will attract a number of birds, which can be great for watching them come and go as well as potentially very calming. Lavender, violets, lamb's ear, mint, honeysuckle and chocolate cosmos will all release beautiful smells when touched or brushed past and lamb's ear is perfect for feel. Edible plants such as mint, evening primrose, basil and rosemary are perfect for accessing all five senses so group them all together.

Wind chimes can create beautiful sounds and also be a great cause-and-effect toy. Pull the cord and it makes a pretty sound. Having a small water feature or a small area for a sandpit or even a few stones is a great way to get your child to focus even for a few moments. The sounds of the water will be very soothing.

Trampolines are great for strengthening the core but are also great for children with ASD, as they find the repetitive bouncing therapeutic. I am not sure what we would do without a trampoline. Dylan bounces on his trampoline every day after school for at least 20 minutes. It's the way he self-regulates himself and he also takes himself off out to it whenever he feels he needs a release.

At first we didn't have much of a garden to have a trampoline so we bought a small indoor one with a bar that he could hold. This was a great way to start and to help build up his core strength as he was a little wobbly. Every time I felt he was getting a little bit over-stimulated I would bring him to the trampoline and help him to bounce. He loved the repetition and I found when he came off it he didn't stim as much. We do have to put a timer on this otherwise I don't think he would stop. When we moved to a house with a bigger garden that was able to have a trampoline in it, I would give him 'brain breaks'. For every 20 minutes on the iPad, we would have to go outside and jump for one minute. He loved being outside and would look up at the sky, smiling. Now, a few years down the line, he can self-regulate and he knows when he needs to go outside and jump. He will go outside and jump and flap his arms and come in a lot happier and calmer.

If you don't the space for a trampoline outside you can, as we did, buy a smaller single trampoline for inside with a bar that they can hold on to for those children who are a little more unstable.

As Dylan gets older, his ASD seems to morph into something else. Things that were a problem when he was two are now no longer a problem, but things that never bothered him before now seem to be a problem. Two steps forward, one step back. Dylan is now seven and we are now getting a little injection of testosterone here and there, and he wants to be a lot more physical. He loves rough-and-tumble play because he loves the pressure sensation on his body, so will often seek that out, but also there are days

Dylan self-regulating
on his trampoline

when he gets really mad and can sometimes hurt others without meaning to. Because of this we have converted our garage into an 'outdoor' playroom for him. This can be done very cheaply and can be done in any space that is a safe space. So no sharp corners or hard things that children can hurt themselves on. We put in a floating floor over the concrete in the garage and took everything out of it. We then laid a rubber matting like ones you would see in a gym or a children's soft play area. We put in a punching bag with some gloves, a roller mat, a peanut-shaped cushion to lie on and lots of therapy putty, balls and some sensory lighting. It's cold and it's raw but it's a place he can go and let off some steam without hurting anyone. By redirecting his aggression, he is much happier in himself. He is learning to self-regulate now and this can be done with all children. I tell Dylan it's totally fine to feel angry, we all feel angry sometimes, it's a human emotion, but we cannot take it out on other people. He is now recognising the signs and tells me or whoever he is with that anger is coming into his brain and then I ask him what he thinks would be a good solution. We have often used a cushion to punch or scream into. Redirecting the anger or frustration helps him feel more in control of himself and his emotions.

Outdoor therapies

ASD children can have difficulty bonding emotionally with others. As a parent of a child with ASD you know that it's hard for your child to make eye contact, communicate what they are feeling and to express themselves to those who they care about. Horse riding, sometimes referred to as equine therapy, is a great way to get your child to experience physical communication without having to use words. They can brush the horse, pat them, hug them and learn how to care for them. They associate the care they provide with feelings and an emotional bridge is constructed. This bond can lead to social and communication skills with others in their life also.

Engaging in equine therapy can also help with your child's way of following directions. It's a fun activity that makes grasping directions easier, as they are motivated to want to make the horse move. Balance and spatial awareness is experienced by riding a horse, providing a gentle natural rhythm. There are many horse-riding schools that specialise in ASD. It can be expensive but there are organisations that can help support children with ASD.

When I first heard of equine therapy I was lucky enough to have a friend (whose child is also on the spectrum) give me a direct report on her child's experience, having recently tried it out. Her child had constant stimming and noise making, but as soon as he sat on a horse and it started to move, the stimming and the noise stopped. He had found his peace. I couldn't wait to try horse riding for Dylan. When we went to the stables Dylan loved the animals and was happy to walk around on this beautiful little pony, but I didn't get the 'Ahhh' moment I think I was searching for. Dylan enjoyed it but it wasn't this magical experience I was hoping for and perhaps expecting.

For children who do a lot of stimming it can really help. Like with all therapies, some will have that magical effect on their children, whereas others like Dylan can just go off in to their own world and not really pay much attention to it at all.

Therapy dogs

Any well-trained family dog can act as a therapy dog. They can be a wonderful calming influence for someone who has ASD. An affectionate dog can provide unconditional love and friendship on a daily basis. Walking the dog provides both with exercise and acts as a social magnet to ease conversation with other children.

The best breeds to consider buying or adopting are golden

Dylan and our dog Mowgli

retrievers, labradors, or labradoodles, as they tend to have a calm temperament and have high intelligence. They can be a full-time job though as well so don't rush in to buying a dog just because it might be good for your child.

There are therapy dogs available for one-to-one sessions as well. These dogs can accompany a child to an appointment or an environment where they might get especially stressed out. Therapy dogs are highly trained and like the dogs for the blind they are allowed to access public areas.

I looked into getting an autism service dog for Dylan but it was hugely expensive and although there are ways to help get funding, either through a Go Fund Me web page or through local charities, we decided to go and buy a puppy. A little mad by anyone's accounts; a toddler, a child with ASD and a young puppy who just wanted to eat everything isn't the best combination and it was a lot of hard work. However, having Dylan help in the process of choosing his puppy and watching him grow with Dylan has been amazing. We have got Mowgli trained now with support from our local community and Dylan loves to just lie beside him. Mowgli has helped with Dylan's anxieties at night-time and knowing Mowgli is in the house has been extremely comforting and reassuring to Dylan.

Swimming

Learning to swim is part of most people's childhoods yet for children with ASD it can be hugely overwhelming. Most swimming pools are loud and have an echo and of course are filled with lots of children. However, if you can find a smaller pool or someone who will be willing to do a lesson at a quieter time it can be wonderfully calming. Water holds the body and makes the body feel weightless. Once Dylan got comfortable with the water and got used to the water splashing his face he absolutely loved it. We found a very patient teacher who helped support Dylan's body in the water and helped him to float. If you are lucky enough to live by the ocean this is also a wonderful place to bring your children. Even just to sit by the ocean and watch the waves come in can be very calming. We actually moved out of London to Brighton so we could be by the sea for Dylan. The sea calms his whole body and mind, it's also a time when Dylan and I can sit and talk about how the sea is feeling that day. If the sea is rough that day Dylan will say the sea is angry and we talk about this emotion and what it means.

Rhian – the speech and language therapist

The outdoors offers a wealth of fun communication and learning. There are so many chance moments. Finding a spider on a drainpipe and re-enacting a favourite 'Incy Wincy Spider' song, generalising it and learning new language concepts such as 'up and down'. Seeing the rain drip off the roof corner and holding your child's hand to run through the drips together, creating shared moments, with the possibility of requesting 'more' for this fun thing to happen over and over again.

To this day, I still feel the joy of a child seeing his first snowfall. Transfixed, he shared protests 'Oh, no, snow is gone' with all the adults in the class as the snow stopped falling. This was a young boy who would often protest through his behaviour by throwing or swiping at whatever was in his reach. This time, motivated and soothed by the snow he took the opportunity to protest in words. We used his outdoor experience to create and stage many further communication opportunities. Bags of flour through a sieve and cans of snow from the pound shop. In fact, these experiences supported him to learn the different possible functions of his words. I talked about the reasons to communicate in Chapter 1 and want to briefly revisit it. If you think about a child using a single word 'go'. It can be used to protest – 'you go and leave me', to request – 'I want to go', to comment – 'look, the car is going' and to question – 'are we going?' One word with so many different communication functions. These functions can be taught by creating motivating opportunities.

The nurseries and school placements that I would consider excellent all encourage outdoor exploration in all weathers. They recognise that nature and seasons create in themselves communication and learning opportunities. From teaching a child to put on hats and scarves, gently encouraging more flexibility in wearing different clothes for a fun purpose, to exposing them to the vocabulary related to these different clothes. Motivation is gained by stimulating different senses. There are some adaptations that can you can consider to enrich these chances even further.

Outdoor zoning

The idea of zoning outdoor play has been a great success in many nurseries. In effect, we already do this on a broader scale in our home and we have been promoting this throughout the book by considering the different functions of your different rooms in your home. It's simply a matter of bringing this idea to the outdoors. This is also talked about in any gardening programme in thinking about and designing your seating, play and plants areas. As ever, for the ASD child this means taking that one step further with more detail and more explicit labelling of areas. The areas that I have seen create the most communication opportunities include water play, messy play, planting, bug/log pile, picnic area for eating and physical/big play (such as balls or a trampoline). I have seen these areas marked by having different mats or surfaces in each and using visual cards stuck to corners or on equipment.

This has the added bonus of reinforcing vocabulary while offering chance opportunities for communication. One example sticks out in my mind.

A communication opportunity

A young boy was desperately trying to take the lid off the sand tray. He tried this by himself for about ten minutes. An adult went over and stood near him, not saying anything. He ripped off the Velcroed symbol and word on the side of the tray and gave it to the adult, making a sound and clearly sending a message of what he wanted. He was quickly given access to the sand and this chance communication was then replicated in many different ways, including: having more sand to request to put in the tray; having a timer to mark the end and putting the lid back on for a quick movement break before getting him to request to remove the lid again.

Messy play

The garden lends itself to messy and sensory play. I have already talked about the traditional tray-based sand and water play. You could extend this play to water balloons and pistols if you are brave! I am always surprised that all sorts of kitchen cupboard favourites can lead to truly fun and motivating mess outdoors: cooked spaghetti with food dye, wet and dry flour with trains making tracks, squirty syringes with blancmange. Often messy food-based play can encourage a gradual exposure to different foods through smell, touch, kissing, licking and taste, as Tara and I talked about in Chapter 3. Other messy play can be based around arts and crafts. Teaching staff I have worked with over the years have inspired all sorts of motivating, creative messy activities. One such inspiration was paint foot baths. Once their feet were coated in paint, children walked up and down plain wallpaper rolls. One boy loved squelching the paint through his toes and, with us only adding paint bit by bit, he requested paint over 20 times in a ten-minute play session. Other ideas include: chalking on pavements, filling a watering can with watery paint and making patterns on a section of big paper, throwing balloon paints at walls lined with newspaper, filling jugs with water and different food colouring and then pouring onto stacked colour cups, and lemonade volcanoes (when you add salt to a recently opened lemonade bottle and watch it explode). These creative pursuits work well for a shared fun experience and you can use this shared/joint attention to support communication as talked about in Chapter 4 about the playroom. You could show your child what to do in a silly, over-the-top way and then give them the opportunity to re-create this by themselves. And if you screw the bottle on the lemonade tight or give a little paint at a time, your child will need to turn to you to ask for help along the way. You can do this through the interpreting and shaping communication attempts discussed above. For example: if your child grabs the coloured bottle, you can interrupt and hold on to it expectantly, looking for them to point or look from the bottle to you and back to the bottle. You can then say 'blue paint' and give it to your child quickly so they link their behaviour with the request, building on their understanding of communication.

Of course, it has to be very motivating for your child to ask and not everyone is motivated by what you or others consider fun. I remember one little girl who I was sure would enjoy my raining flour from a great height onto black paper and then drawing. She didn't. She turned away and starting snapping some twigs behind her. Next time I tried building a thunderstorm of dry spaghetti, by pouring the spaghetti into baking trays and then smashing it up. She much preferred this harder and louder activity.

Social games with rules

The garden is the perfect place to practise simple games that you will see played out in playtimes and parks around the globe. Consider what you know about your child's preferred type of play (see Chapter 4) and then choose a game they may be interested in.

Choosing a game

Physical play
Chase/tag
Using playground apparatus (roundabout/seesaw)
Hopscotch

Sensory play
Obstacle courses over different surfaces
Outdoor musical instruments (upturned buckets, shouting through old drainpipes)
Ring-a-ring-a-roses (going fast, round and round, re-creating the feeling of spinning)

Cause-and-effect play
Musical bumps
Pass the parcel
Catch the ball, or kick or throw the ball into a hoop

Symbolic play with rules
What's the time, Mr Wolf?
Mother May I
Simon Says

These will have the added bonus of helping your child prepare for children's parties and school playground games.

You can teach these through repeated exposure and modelling, as well as through different levels of prompting and Social Stories™ or video modelling. You could make a simple set of sequenced photographs explaining the game. You would look at these together while saying simple phrases or sentences. For example: music on and people dance (photo of play button on phone and people dancing); music stops and people sit (photo of stop button on phone and people sitting). Remember your child has to be able to share some attention and show an understanding of photos for this strategy to work.

Gardening

There is a volume of evidence showing the positive therapeutic impact that gardening offers for anxiety and mental health difficulties. As we know, anxiety is an emotion often experienced by children with ASD. I believe that connecting to nature and being outdoors, and the physical and sensory aspects of the gardening experience, are of great benefit. Tara has explored the sensory garden and plants to provide stimulation and/or calming for the five senses. I want to talk a little more about the possibility of teaching your child words in the garden.

Once your child has understood the process of communication – that it is to send a message from one person to another for needs or to share experiences – they begin to learn vocabulary. Children will understand many more words, hundreds of them, before they speak a single one. Typically, children first understand words that are used often in everyday circumstances such as social greetings or requests for 'more' or to be picked 'up'. Children then learn concrete words that they hear lots and lots such as 'car' or 'mummy'. Later they expand their understanding of these familiar concrete words and will start to use up to 20 words as well as start to understand instructions used in the everyday such as 'give me' and 'all gone'. Children then have an explosion in understanding, developing an internal vocabulary of 200–500 words. They will also start to understand simple questions and say simple sentences. Children who are learning language in a disordered way (not simply being delayed in reaching the different stages but actually going about the learning differently) will develop through this vocabulary uniquely. At times they will seem to leap with their words but either not maintain these words or not use them correctly. Understanding some principles to help children expand their understanding and use of words will only benefit this process.

- Pick the words you are going to focus on for a few weeks and share these with family, friends and nursery/school.

- Offer repeated exposure: saying the words many, many times (a child having language difficulties needs to hear the word so many more times than the child without any difficulty).

- Bridge word learning with an area of strength. This is often visual, for example, making pictures for your focused words and sharing these with all involved with your child.

- Link the words with real-life experiences and then practise, practise, practise.

Now let us consider the natural communication opportunities offered through gardening using the principles above. You first select the words such as 'water' and 'grass'. You work on the understanding through exposure linked to a task that your child is also focused on, by saying the word over and over as you are both doing the activity: 'Water on the grass, water on the flowers, water on the soil, water on the pavement.' You can also link in with your pre-prepared visual pictures, asking your child to find the water/grass pictures, which you then match with the watering can or a patch of grass. Once you have worked on their understanding of these words you can also work on your child using them. This might be by creating opportunities for them to request the water or grass (you watering the garden or throwing bits of the grass into the air). Or, as you play with the visuals, you could arrange to find numerous copies of the pictures hidden around the garden. Then say these words as you post them through your home's letter box. It's best to have these natural garden communication sessions little and often throughout your week rather than for one long session. And, in my experience, you have to plan them into your family life or these chances will get lost in the 101 things to do.

You can also consider nature beyond your garden, I have really enjoyed class trips to farms, zoos and nature trails. In Chapter 9, you will find references for useful information about engaging children with the natural environment and some examples of ASD-specific guides and publications for walks and nature trails. In addition to this, on any of your outdoor nature trips, you can make a personal photo book or album on your phone or iPad. You can then look at these together after the experience which will continue to support vocabulary development.

Option book for outdoors

Not every moment needs to be a moment of learning or therapy. In my experience children will often need some time to do what comes without an interaction or learning challenge. This may involve what is often referred to as self-stimulating behaviour, for example flapping hands or stepping around repetitively in a certain pattern. However, after too much time of a highly repetitive activity, some children can become distressed. This can then make transitioning from this activity to another difficult. Sometimes even with clearly staged play areas and lots of available motivating toys, children can be unsure of what to do, for how long to do these things and what will be coming next. A simple picture book of all the outdoor activities and a board with three to six numbers can help. The child can choose from the book what they want to do, put these pictures against their numbers and play these for a time, taking these off the board when finished. They can work through their choices for garden time while also having some leftover time to do the repetitive activity they enjoy.

Yoga and mindfulness

This is something that recently many parents and schools have been investigating. The theory is that practising yoga poses may provide some of the sensory stimulation sought by people with ASD while also helping people be focused and present, soothing stress and anxiety. In general children will need to be able to copy actions in order to access this fully. However, if children do not mind being touched and directed into different positions they may still enjoy it.

The teaching of mindfulness can be of benefit for some individuals with ASD. However, there is even more growing evidence to suggest it can be effective in reducing parental stress. A less stressed parent can better cope with some of their children's behavioural challenges. I would encourage you to investigate this for yourself but it will not be for everyone.

I hope you will look to the outdoors as a motivating place full of natural and creative learning.

OUT AND ABOUT

Tara – the mum

Going out is part of life. Whether we are popping to the shops or picking up children from school, it has to be done. I know it can be daunting taking your child out, but with a little forward thinking and planning it can be enjoyable for all.

Car travel

Having a visual timetable in the car can help with anxieties about where you are going. So if you have a few pictures of where you are going it will help. I also keep a pen and paper in the car just in case the plan unexpectedly changes. Once, we were on our way to the zoo and the car engine blew up and we were stuck on the side of the road. Dylan had been looking forward to going to the zoo for so long, and I knew we were still going to go; however, how we got to the zoo was going to change. So I took out a pen and paper, drew six squares and drew in the new agenda for the day, labelled one to six. He then knew that the end goal was still going to be the same but that we needed to take a detour or two along the way.

Whether your child is verbal or non-verbal, having a visual will help them understand what is going on. Luckily Dylan took his new schedule without having any meltdowns and we did get to the zoo even if it was a few hours later.

Setting a new timetable in a hurry

I also keep a bag of goodies just for the car: different interesting toys that he only plays with in the car.

Shopping

Taking your child shopping is one thing a parent may dread doing whether their child has ASD or not. As I said in Chapter 2, 'The Bedroom', getting your child to wear new clothes or any clothes at all can be a big issue. Allowing your child to pick and choose their own clothes can be beneficial and give the child more control over what they can wear. I try to find shops that are not in big brightly lit malls, instead focusing on outlet stores where I can park right outside. I take photos of the shop and its layout before we go and show it to Dylan so he knows what to expect. It's also worth phoning up the shop a day before to explain you have a child with ASD and ask if it would be possible for them to open the shop five minutes before they actually open so you can browse with your little one without other people around. Also it's worth asking in advance if they could get three or four jumpers or whatever item you are looking for in whatever size you are looking for and putting them in a big dressing room for you. That way when you arrive they are already put aside for you and you can both go through the clothes, touching them and smelling them. Keep it brief, no more than 15 minutes.

After your shopping trips, reward your child with a treat, so it becomes a pleasant experience for them.

School run

This is something that I know stresses a lot of parents out. Whether you have a child in school or you need to drop older children at school, it is always a worry. Have a chat to your school about your child's needs and see what they can do to accommodate you. Perhaps they have a car park that you can park in? Most schools are very inclusive and are happy to help. If your child is at a mainstream school, try dropping them off ten minutes earlier and picking them up ten minutes earlier to avoid the rush of schoolchildren. That way they can enter the classroom first and settle down before the morning liveliness.

I am going to touch on the subject of school as there are many different options for your child and this can become a little overwhelming. What is right for one child might not be right for someone else as the spectrum is so varied. You know your child the best so always follow your gut instinct, even if your gut instinct changes halfway through the school year, like mine did.

There are specialist settings, base units and, of course, mainstream school. Dylan has been to all three and now, after a few years in each, we have successfully transitioned him into a mainstream school with full-time support.

Dylan started off at a specialist nursery setting, which was solely geared up to help him with his ASD. They organised all the speech therapists and occupational therapists and it was all built into his schedule, which saved us from having to take him to a million and one appointments. They also helped me with toilet training and gave me a lot of great advice that I have used throughout this book. After he graduated from his specialist setting they advised me on where they thought Dylan would be best suited to go. We decided on sending him to a base unit, which is an ASD unit attached to a mainstream school. The children can integrate as much or as little as the teachers feel they can handle into a mainstream school. It is a very gentle way of introducing them to a mainstream school.

What we found for Dylan though was that halfway through the school year, he could tolerate mainstream school but the school itself was too big and that was hard for him so he spent more and more time in the base unit. Dylan loves to have friends and although he needed help communicating and needed a lot of help in the classroom itself to complete his tasks, we decided to move him to a mainstream school. We as a family actually moved out of London down to Brighton as I found a beautiful small village school for Dylan. They were very welcoming and have really been open to a lot of ideas that I had taken from the base unit to help Dylan in a mainstream setting. The school's SENCO (Special Educational Needs Co-ordinator) should be able to help families apply for additional help while at the school. For a child with an Education, Health and Care Plan, in the UK, the school receives additional money from the government. The SENCO, working with parents and school management, can plan how to use these additional funds to best support the child. Dylan has a full-time one-to-one with him at all times of the school day who helps him to complete his work tasks, be it in the classroom or in a small group working outside of the classroom. The school have been fantastic and have allowed Dylan to have a small, one-man trampoline in the school so that when he needs a 'brain break' he can take a five-, ten- or 15-minute 'time out' card to go and regulate himself. He also has a tent in his classroom so if he becomes overwhelmed he goes in there and takes a time out. Dylan also has ear defenders in his bag which he puts on at lunch time when he goes into the noisy hall. He can sit with his friends and still be part of everything but in a more comfortable environment for him. Dylan also keeps a fidget bag at his desk as he can become very distracted in class and feels the need to move around or do something. In his fidget bag he has some therapeutic putty, some dice, a stretchy man that you can contort into different shapes and a special pen that he can use.

Air travel

Going through airports as smoothly as possible is going to take military-style organisation. Phone your airline ahead of time to tell them what you require. Ask if they have a family or disability entrance you can use. Most airports offer assistance; you just need to phone up in advance. You can get a golf buggy to your gate and most airports do have a quick pass entrance to get through security.

Before you leave home, have pictures printed out of your destination and have your child's checklist ready for them to tick off once steps are completed. For example: taxi, pick up bags, check in, etc.

Leave home in plenty of time to allow for any meltdowns that might happen along the way. It's also worth making sure your child is in a tracksuit and slippers to avoid being told to take off your shoes going through security.

Headphones or ear defenders can be brilliant in this instance as there are so many unexpected noises and bright lights at airports. If you sense your child is starting to get anxious, find a quiet space and give them something that calms them down like an iPad or something to get their minds off whatever is causing them to get anxious. Then when you feel they are ready, proceed forward. Once on the plane, again having a small bag of toys for them to play with will distract them.

Family outings

One of the hardest things I found about having a child with ASD was not for me but for Luca. I am constantly reminded every day that life is different for him, than if he had not had a sibling with ASD. For Luca he knows no different. He loves and adores his big brother but things can be tough for him. Not so long ago we were going through airport security and a security guard who was being very sweet got the camera down to Dylan's eye level

Dylan and his little brother Luca

and took a photo of him without warning. This sent Dylan into a panic which resulted in a meltdown. While Andrew tried to hold Dylan and get him to a safe quiet place (which as you can imagine is hard going through airport security as you cannot go back) I picked up all the bags and trail of clothes left behind. Luca, who is only three, picked up his bag and Dylan's and trundled along behind me. As we followed Andrew and Dylan, Luca was explaining to the security guards that this was his big brother and he was just feeling a little angry and sad, but not to worry because he would be OK. I looked at my little red-headed boy with tears prickling behind my eyes. I was so proud of him for understanding and for helping me, when usually he is the one bolting away from me in excitement. He knows that when Dylan is having a moment Mummy's focus will be taken away from him and given to his brother. This is hard.

It is also harder for older siblings to understand, as they may remember a time before ASD and their worlds have been changed. With a lot of families I talk to this is a concern for them. Their older children may start acting up as a result of feeling 'forgotten' or ask 'Why can't we go to the cinema together?'

It's also very common for the mums to stay at home with the child with ASD and the dads to take the older siblings off. This can create divide among families and can lead to resentment. I did this for a long time. I thought that Andrew could not handle Dylan's meltdowns and we would quite often pair off: Dylan and I, Luca and Andrew. This caused problems between Andrew and myself, but also between Andrew and Dylan or myself and Luca. Luca started to get anxious when Andrew wasn't here. And his behaviour started to change. He also started hitting Dylan to get attention from me.

I soon realised that Luca also needed me. Yes, he could talk and communicate with me, but that didn't mean he didn't need me. He is three. So we started doing things more as a family and I also took Luca out of nursery one morning a week so we could do some things together without Andrew or Dylan. This helped our relationship no end.

Going out together as a family and bonding is so important. Thankfully more and more people are becoming more aware of ASD and are making it easier to go on family outings. Most cinemas now offer an autism-friendly screening once a month, usually on the first Sunday of every month. This is one of our favourite pastimes as a family, as we can sit there and not feel the need to apologise for Dylan's behaviours and getting up and down out of his seat. The lights are on so it's not dark and they turn the sound down lower so it's not so sensory overloading.

This is great for the whole family as younger siblings also get a free pass for having wriggling bums and older siblings get to see their favourite film with their family and will also see other families like theirs and not feel so isolated.

Most theme parks have a special pass, which allows you to skip the queue and go straight to the front. Most children with ASD love the motion of rides; it's also a great time for all the children to do something fun together. I always phone ahead and ask if they have a quick queue system for the tickets as well. Or I just buy them online, which can sometimes be cheaper and saves time.

Top tip

Most attractions also let the carer of the person with ASD in for free, so always mention you have a child with ASD. Many councils and states issue a carers' card and a card that proves your child's needs so you can keep this in your wallet and show it to cinemas, theme parks, etc.

Rhian – the speech and language therapist

Tara has explored many different aspects of getting out and about, talking about her experiences that may give you some ideas.

I want to narrow the focus and think about two main themes: meltdowns and communicating with others outside the home. These themes cover the common challenges that parents over the years have shared with me, commenting that having an ASD child can mean being at home more because of the fear. The fear of the what-ifs. The dread of the battle with the reluctant child to even get out the door. Often young people with ASD can hold on strongly to previous negative experiences. These past negative experiences can be triggered by a similar situation and fully relived again and again, negatively influencing future outings. This builds up general resistance and contributes to meltdowns. The fear parents feel is also linked to how to deal with these potential or, in many cases guaranteed, meltdowns.

The meltdowns

The anxiety from both parent and child can begin to build a long time before stepping out the door. There are numerous anticipated and real difficulties related to getting out and about, from the safety of your child to the possible judgement from others if there is a meltdown. All of which can make the process very difficult or indeed even prevent you and your family from going out.

I will echo Tara's call for forward thinking and planning. As a parent, you already have experience of doing this with nappy bags, a change of clothes, snacks and toys. However, this planning and preparation needs a turbo charge with ASD in mind.

It is useful to practise this turbo planning and preparing for a specific family outing. This could be the weekly supermarket shop or an anticipated special family meal out in a restaurant. The planning can start weeks in advance. In this planning, ask yourself these questions:

- *Can you aim to select the right place for you and your child?* This isn't foolproof but start by thinking about what you know about your child. Consider their sensory preferences that were previously discussed in Chapter 2. What is it that they may find difficult about a trip? Could it be the bright lights or crowds or places where sounds are amplified or echo? Armed with this knowledge and the knowledge of the area you live or want to visit, can you think of somewhere where there may be fewer challenges for your child? For example, for the child who doesn't like crowds or noise go to a smaller restaurant with carpet. Or for the child who likes a lot of space go to a supermarket that has wide aisles with a familiar layout.

- *Can you prepare for the visit through gradual exposure to the place and event?* This could be by looking at photos, leaflets or even the Facebook pages or adverts about the venue together.

- *Can you make a visit within your day routine?* This could be just to pass by it or maybe to step inside, but without the full task of shopping or eating.

- *Can you communicate to your child what to expect from the experience?* This would mean providing information around the sequence. This can involve showing pictures or photos of the steps in the event or experience. For example, 'First we drive to the café, then we find a table, we look at the menu, we order food, we wait and eat the food when it comes, we then pay and drive home.' Tara has talked about having a pen and paper to help deal with changes to any plan when they are out and about. I cannot recommend this enough. In my experience a small whiteboard with wipeable pens is an invaluable and portable tool. This provides visual reassurance and explanation when words are often the hardest to understand, especially when anxiety is involved.

Now even with all this planning, I guarantee you, on occasion, it will still be hard for you and your child. Meltdowns will occur. Of course, first and foremost, you have to keep your child safe. If they are running out into the road you may have to act before you think. There may, however, be some preventative measures around safety you can take. I have seen parents use the backpack with reins, standing boards on prams and even adult scooters with the child on the front in attempts to keep some physical control and zones of safety. I also know parents who have purposefully chosen to go to shopping centres with double security doors as an extra measure to make an escape more difficult.

The EarlyBird or a similar parenting course will help you explore different tools/approaches to analyse your child's behaviours and adjust your plans accordingly. One of the tools that is used to consider behaviour is the iceberg analogy, with the behaviour you see being only the tip of the iceberg with a host of reasons for that behaviour being the mass that lies under the surface of the sea. In order to understand the behaviour at the tip you have to delve below the surface. These discoveries can further help your planning for the next outing, bearing in mind that all behaviour serves a function. Therefore, rather than ignore undesired behaviours, you seek to understand them.

Say you are in the middle of a meltdown, but your child is safe. What should you do? At times I think the only thing to do is wait it out. This can be hard and frustrating.

Some parents have shared that giving out a card (see Chapter 9) saying 'This person is on the autism spectrum' can help them feel a sense of control if they do not want to explain to strangers what is happening. It also has the added bonus of educating the general public. However, I do understand that many of you would not wish to share or discuss this at all with strangers.

In groups parents have opened up about their experiences around their child's challenging behaviour when they are out and about. They talked about people looking at them with a sense of judgement. They have reported that people say things like 'You are amazing, I just don't know how you do it' and that as parents they often feel this is code for 'How do you live your life? And I am glad I'm not you.' Parents have also talked about how people – family, friends and strangers alike will ask 'Where on the spectrum is he?' This is one of the most common questions I get asked when parents attend a diagnosis appointment. It is also the question I feel I do not answer as parents would expect or indeed want. From my own experience and from discussions with autistic adults, thinking in terms of plotting the autism on the spectrum is not always helpful, as it does not go on to provide useful information. In fact, as pointed out to me one day by a young man who was told he was mildly autistic, this description is not correct, because 'mildly autistic' implied that his core symptoms (regarding social communication, relationships and flexibility of thought) for ASD were mild. They were not. He had significant needs related to how he understands social situations and develops relationships. Rather, this 'mild' description was related to his thinking and language skills. This is similar to the term 'high functioning'. We often talk about ASD in this way because the people we are talking about have good language skills. They can complete complex puzzles or cognitive tasks. Their cognitive skills as far as we can measure by static assessments are shown to be within a normal range or may be even slightly higher than the normal range. Yet it may be that at that moment in their life their ASD is all consuming, preventing them from leaving the house or being able to stay in a lesson. Therefore, they are actually not functioning at all well.

The author, David Mitchell, who has a son with ASD, explored this in an article he wrote for *The Guardian* (see Chapter 9 for details). He commented that describing his son in these terms is equal to picking a colour from the rainbow. So, when people ask him what kind of autism his son has, or where he is on the spectrum, he may as well respond that today he has yellow autism. The current thinking as directed by our diagnostic guidelines is that it is best to think of autism in terms of the support needed. Whether this is minimal adaptations, some additional support or a high level of support. However, for this to work we have to be fluid in these descriptors, moving according to the child's needs at different points in his life. ASD is a dynamic difficulty. At times, your child may need no support as they are settled in class, have one or two friends and are joining in family life. At other times they may need to move to a high level of support because they have started a new school or their sensory world has become too overwhelming. This is very difficult for education and health services to respond to. Services are often planned for and linked in with a child on an annual basis not always allowing for this fluidity. This way of thinking also requires an overhaul in how we see ASD, as not something to normalise and cure but rather as a developmental difference.

Parents have reflected with me that an important point of learning has been to understand the fight/flight/freeze theory. This has helped them manage their own expectations of a child during a meltdown. The fight/flight/freeze response is an instinct that we all have: a primitive response to fear. A way to protect ourselves from danger and ensure our survival. Confusingly, this response, even when invoked, can be controlled by many of us, as we are able to think through a situation and why in this instance it is OK. An example might be when you have to have an invasive procedure at the dentist's or doctor's surgery. Although you are being touched and handled in an intimate and sometimes painful way, you can reason that this is in your best interest. Your child with ASD cannot always engage these thinking skills and so they can act in a more subconscious and instinctual way. On top of this, an ASD child will have so many more possible triggers, as they experience the world differently both in a sensory and social way. You may see your child lash out, kick, bite, scream or simply bolt as fast as they can. Your child is experiencing physical changes in this time. An increased heart rate, drop in glucose level and consequent surge of adrenalin. You may see them sweating, breathing fast and hard. They may report tingly cold hands or feet as blood is directed to the big organs. There is an overall state of confusion with it being hard to think. Neuroscience has found evidence on the impact of emotion on the physical side as just described as well as other brain functions such as vision, memory, understanding and using language. This means that reasoning and distracting during this period is not always the best way to go because the capacity for your children to process and understand this may well be reduced. In my experience, the calming period can be anywhere from 5 minutes to 45 minutes. This is hard to endure but parents have shared that understanding this process can help them 'weather it or buckle down through it'. This understanding has also made them more confident that creating a safe place to calm, even when out and about, is appropriate, whether this is under a scarf or by taking their child into a big squeeze.

I want to add a warning here. Try to be careful when using touch or any restraint on your child. You should try to keep hands off children especially when they are upset. Touch at this time can be viewed as an act of aggression and further escalate a situation. So try to avoid it unless you are certain it has a calming influence.

Parents have said that understanding this process makes them more confident in giving their child the calm box discussed in Chapters 1 and 6. This understanding helps them brush off the possible judgement of others who might think that they are rewarding this behaviour. Parents have also given themselves permission to move on and come back to the learning about the incident, when they are able to think about it in a safer space with a cup of tea. They can then analyse the incident in more depth and think through whether there is anything they could do differently going forward, leading up to, during or after the meltdown. I often say the only behaviour we can control is our own. This is not to say you cannot actively plan for and change what you do in order to influence the behaviour of your child.

I often hear parents comment that if their child could only communicate their frustrations, the meltdowns would disappear. However, take a moment to think about this.

A young boy who is very rigid wants to access the same toy in the same way over and over. He snatches it from others. He kicks and bites when prevented from having it. If he could use his words to say 'I want that toy', or if he could understand the words 'no' or 'not now as your brother is playing', do you think he would stop snatching or kicking?

In some cases, maybe; but in my experience, it is often the impairment in flexible thinking and seeing things from others' viewpoints that is leading to this behaviour rather than his difficulty understanding words and communicating what he wants.

I am not saying you cannot work on these difficulties. I am saying that working on controlling the environment, for example giving clear timed turns as marked by a stopwatch, could be the most effective starting point. I also want to highlight that even when or if your child talks they are likely to continue to find things challenging and sometimes show this through their behaviours. Nevertheless, I certainly believe that improved communication skills will impact positively on behaviour.

Your child communicating with others outside of the home

Some parents have to trust in guessing or, if at times they are more certain, in interpreting their child's individual sets of behaviours, sounds and movements as meaningful communication. This is all the more challenging and pressurised when out and about.

This, along with so many other reasons, places communication firmly upfront in the queue of skills to develop. Ideally communication targets should be set with you and your child (if they are able to take part). Many parents understandably will often want their child to talk. Some will acknowledge that, although this remains the hope, they would settle for 'any successful communication system that is understood by others'. There are increasingly more options with what we call augmentative (supporting) and alternative communication (AAC) systems. There are various options:

- *No-tech systems*. This is simply what you have available on you right now to support what you say. This means you can use body language, gesture and facial expression. Think of the parent saying 'no' to a crawling baby about to head to the stairs. Standing with feet apart, shaking their head slowly, finger wagging and extending the start of the word leading into a very firm-sounding word. We often use these supports with a baby or very young child. If your child is at a very early stage of development, that is, if they are crying or shouting as a reflex to being hurt or sad but not directing this to you to share or communicate, try to consciously up the use of your body, gesture and facial expression to highlight your words. Remember to keep your communication to very simple words or statements.

- *Low-tech systems.* These are non-electronic systems and can include communication boards, PECS and choosing boards. Think of the parent at the ice-cream van holding up their young toddler, looking at the board of pictures and asking them to choose what they want. If your child is beginning to understand that their behaviour tells you a message and you see some intentional communication through actions, sounds or words, these are worth exploring. For example, they may put their hands up while making a sound to tell you 'I want to be picked up' or they may hand you a ball and look at the tower to tell you 'knock it over again'. In Chapter 3 we briefly explored how to support children to tell us about pain and discomfort, I want to take a moment to talk a little bit more about the use of a pain scale. This can be used in the home when your child has hurt themselves and out and about to help with the doctor's/ dentist/hospital. An adult version is the Abbey Pain Scale and it is a visual system, pointing to parts of the body and then using a scale. This obviously takes a level of symbolic understanding and needs to be taught. You can start with online modelling, commenting and linking a hurt picture when others are hurt. You can look at pictures or cartoons of people hurting themselves, pausing these and referring to the pain scale. When you know the part of your child that is hurt you can link this to the pain scale. I strongly believe this is an area we all need to work on – parents and all the professionals involved. I have encountered many stories about hospital or GP visits where it has been difficult to work out what is wrong and in some cases the child's physical health is worsened or deteriorates because they haven't had words or ways to express pain or illness. Of course, this is not a magic solution and while the system is being implemented but in fact the child is not yet ready for it, we have to go back to observation and interpretations. Carrying the personal passport, discussed in Chapter 1, to appointments is useful here. Signs you may see to indicate pain often include changes in behaviour whether this is your child becoming more agitated or more passive. Hospitals should have a learning disability nurse or advocate so do ask. We have to help others in the community to see past the ASD and quirks as the go-to explanation for all behaviours; instead look deeper to find out what these may be telling us.

- *Light-tech systems (sometimes referred to as mid-tech systems).* These are still non-electronic but include battery-operated systems such as single switch voice output Big Macs. As before, if your child is starting to make intentional and direct sounds, actions and words and has some emerging understanding of cause-and-effect play, these may be useful to think about. In my experience these can provide motivation to join in group or class activities in a simple way. These can also enhance the understanding that doing something results in getting something, which is the basic premise for communication. Think about a child who loves deep pressure practising hitting a button that says 'hug me' which results in an immediate squeeze. They start to link hitting the button with the reward.

- *High-tech devices.* These are electronic and are power charged. They are dynamic. People often need some training to use them successfully. They can include things such as voice output devices or speech-generated systems and specialist software on iPad devices. Think of the child that comes up to you and consistently says a particular sound which you understand as a request for a drink. Alternatively, the child who opens and closes her hands while looking at you meaning she wants you to sing 'Twinkle Twinkle'. If your child has an understanding of the communication process, that is, it involves sending a message to another person, or if they have a number of ways or possibly even a personalised system of sharing communication, you may want to talk to the speech and language therapist and the team around your child to explore high-tech devices.

Parents often come to my sessions explaining that their child is good at using technology and they want to try high-tech communication systems. This is logical. However, there is a difference between being able to play games or complete activities by yourself for yourself on technology and using this same technology to communicate with another person. The difference is intention: the intention to share and communicate. Often the low-tech devices teach this intention. I believe that these low-tech devices can have the same impact as high-tech devices in increasing communication effectiveness and engagement.

From reading this book so far, I hope you will recognise that a wide range of approaches are advocated to support ASD children develop to the best of their own ability. I think it is a missed opportunity when the use of supported communication systems is discouraged. There is no evidence to suggest AAC systems prevent speech from developing.

The foundations for communication and consequently for an AAC system to succeed can be laid through working on:

- *Social motivation/joint attention*. Does your child enjoy some interactions with another, and can you build on the number and length of time spent on these fun, motivating moments?

  You can do this through the previously mentioned 'intensive interaction': copy your child's actions and sounds or play with objects (having your own set) with the expectation that they look to you and share some attention. You can play games that need another person in order to be successful. These can be singing or movement based (rocking/spinning/tickles). You can think about the play principles of including your child's interests, as discussed above.

- *Intentional communication*. Does your child understand cause and effect with objects?

  Play with toys that promote this understanding such as pop-up toys or wind-up toys. You are working on them anticipating something is going to happen by pressing or pushing to make it happen. Does your child understand cause and effect with play/communication? Practise waiting/pausing during sequences of play with you. For example, when you stamp both feet down and extend your hands, does your child reach out, understanding spinning is about to start? Practise waiting/pausing in a motivating song or game and look for behaviour, a reach, a point or facial expression/eye contact that can be interpreted as them sending a message that they want a turn.

- *Reasons to communicate*. Do you know your child's likes and dislikes?

  Observe and record these during your day-to-day life or from your staged playrooms and then if possible re-create these opportunities again and again in your home or out and about.

- *Complexity.* Is your child having opportunities to choose or request the things they like?

  Provide environmental supports/cues by labelling cupboards with the things inside and even putting labels on play equipment such as tightly screwed-on bubble mixture pots. Try putting things they like out of reach or ease of access and positioning yourself close by to prompt any chance communication.

  You can model matching objects to pictures or gestures in everyday routines and during fun games.

  You can offer lots and lots of choices between objects and, if appropriate, photos/symbols.

Please do explore AAC with the speech and language therapist involved with your child. Not only does this need to be considered in the context of your individual child's communication profile but also in terms of other factors that can impact on its success, such as having someone to communicate with who has the knowledge and means to support the use of the system.

THE OFFICE

Tara and Rhian

In this chapter, rather than talking about a particular room or setting, we will offer an additional, easy-to-navigate list of resources to signpost you to additional information to explore. Some of these have been talked about throughout the book and some of these we have found useful along the way in our discovery of ASD.

We would always encourage you to first speak to the team working with you and your ASD child, whether this is as follow-up after their diagnosis, within their nursery or from specific outreach services. The team will have a wealth of information to share. Nothing can replace a face-to-face chat with someone about your individual child.

Apps

There are many apps, some of which are very expensive. Some are specifically linked to developing augmentative or alternative communication systems for your child. We would recommend, if you are interested in these, that you talk to the team involved with your child to explore whether this technology would suit your child's individual needs. We will signpost you to apps that we have found useful and that are free or cheap.

Helpful to practise social situations

FindMe (Autism)

Model Me Going Places

Social Stories™ creator and library at the Touch Autism website: http://touchautism.com/app/social-stories-creator-library

Helpful to work on understanding cause and effect

ReacTickles

Talking Tom Cat

Helpful to work on activities of daily living

See Me Go Potty

Sleepy Sounds

For the 'wonkidos going potty' animation, as mentioned in Chapter 5, see www.wonkido.com.

For discussion around appropriate screen time you can download an article at www.screenfree.org/wp-content/uploads/2014/01/screentimefs.pdf.

Communication and interaction

There are so many resources, often matched to the ages and stages of your child's development and life. We will mention more general sources of information.

You can read more about the means, reasons and opportunity model for communication in this article: Money, D. and Thurman, S. (1994) 'Talkabout Communication.' *Bulletin of the College of Speech and Language Therapists 504*, 12–13.

For information related to general tips and the attention levels discussed in Chapter 4: Cooper, J., Moodley, M. and Reynell, J. (1978) *Helping Language Development*. London: Hodder Arnold.

For a contact point and to explore training opportunities on the intervention model offering the irresistible invitation to learn, see the Attention Autism section by Gina Davies at http:// ginadavies.co.uk.

A book which will support you to understand your child's general stage of functional communication, provide ideas for targets to work towards, and arm you with both general principles and activities to do with your child: Sussman, F. (1999) *More Than Words: Helping Parents Promote Communication and Social Skills in Children with Autism Spectrum Disorder*. Available at www.hanen. org/Guidebooks---DVDs/Parents/More-Than-Words.aspx.

For information about the origin of Social Stories™ and possible workshops to attend, see the Carol Gray Social Stories™ website: https://carolgraysocialstories.com/social-stories.

A book packed with Social Stories™ for everyday life with a CD for free printable resources: Gray, C. (2015) *The New Social Story Book*. Arlington, TX: Future Horizons Incorporated.

A useful resource book to guide you in writing your own Social Stories™ unique to your child's needs with lots of useful examples: Williams, C. and Wright, B. (2016) *A Guide to Writing Social Stories*. London: Jessica Kingsley Publishers.

Model Me Kids is an online resource for video modelling with links to research backing the approach, YouTube videos and further useful tools to invest in: www.modelmekids.com.

For information on PECS and links to dates for specific training in PECS (Pyramid Educational Consultants offers services worldwide): http://pecs.com and http://pecs-unitedkingdom.com.

Communication Passports (in association with CALL Scotland) provides communication passport templates to fill in and/or adapt for others to get to know your child and how they communicate: www.communicationpassports.org.uk/Creating-Passports/Templates.

My Hospital Passport by the National Autistic Society provides a 'passport' for those children who are needing hospital treatment: www.autism.org.uk/about/health/hospital-passport.aspx.

Face Legs Activity Cry Consolability (FLACC) is a behavioural scale you can download for young children and those children who are non-verbal: www.mghpcs.org/eed_portal/Documents/Pain/Pediatric/FLACC_scale.pdf

Another tool for considering levels of pain is the Abbey Pain Scale. Although not specifically designed for ASD, nor for parents, it can be a useful scale to consider non-verbal behaviours indicating possible pain. It can also be useful to share with medical professionals: www.wales.nhs.uk/sitesplus/documents/862/FOI-286f-13.pdf.

Visiting the Doctor is a page full of useful information and links to resources that will support you and your child in visiting medical professionals and getting the right care based on their needs: www.autism.org.uk/about/health/doctor.aspx.

Do2Learn is a website packed with free downloadable symbols for visual timetables, routines of the day, learning about emotions and social skills and supporting behaviour: www.do2learn.com.

Diagnosis

There is variation within and across countries with the exact process involved in diagnosing your child's ASD. However, the following health information and guidelines should help you understand the path and broad services available (albeit services are presented in very different ways according to the local services for your child):

NHS information: www.nhs.uk/Conditions/Autistic-spectrum-disorder/Pages/Diagnosis.aspx.

Guidelines for clinical services from a non-departmental public body: www.nice.org.uk/guidance/cg170.

Education access and support

Education access should be universal as indicated by children's international rights and, additionally, equality, diversity and disability law. For information on human rights and the United Nations Convention on the Rights of the Child, with articles on the rights not to be discriminated against and to receive an education: www.nidirect.gov.uk/articles/childrens-human-rights.

An Act detailing support available for children and young people in England with special educational needs or disabilities: Part 3 of the Children and Families Act 2014: www.legislation.gov.uk/ukpga/2014/6/part/3/enacted.

An Act that strengthens the requirement of partnership between different agencies for the benefit of a child: the Children Act 2004 amended from 1989: www.legislation.gov.uk/ukpga/2004/31/contents.

An Act that supports children with disability in education, ensuring children are not discriminated against because of their disability: the Equality Act 2010: www.legislation.gov.uk/ukpga/2010/15/section/6.

Education support will differ according to your child's individual profile or needs and strengths as well as the country you are in. However, if you are in the UK, the Acts above, especially the Equality Act, serve to promote disability rights for your child to access wellbeing and education. There are free and impartial services run in many places across the UK that can help you understand the law, offer support for your child and work towards resolution in cases of disagreement. These include:

Special Educational Needs and Disabilities Information, Advice and Support Service: https://councilfordisabledchildren.org.uk/information-advice-and-support-services-network/find-your-local-ias-service.

SNAP Cymru : a national charity unique to Wales supporting inclusion: www.snapcymru.org.

Special Education Needs Advice Centre
(Northern Ireland): www.senac.co.uk.

Emotions

If you want to read more about the stages of grief explored in Chapter 1: Kübler-Ross, E. (1997 reprint) *On Death and Dying.* New York: Simon & Schuster.

There are a plethora of fantastic resources to help typically developing as well as children with ASD understand their own and others' emotions. We will only touch on a few we have found particularly useful.

Support for learning emotional vocabulary and recognising emotions in others, through matching, sorting and explaining

You can make your own dominoes to practise labelling emotions over and over at Emotional Resources 4 Kids: www. emotionalresources4kids.com/emotional-domino.

Alternatively, you can buy the Emotion-oes game from Amazon.

You can make your own sorting game from visuals provided by Twinkl: www.twinkl.co.uk/resource/t-s-1057-happy-sad-and-angry-sorting-activity.

There are also free printable resources from Do2Learn: www. do2learn.com.

As with previously mentioned resources, you don't have to make them; you can choose to buy some cards. We have found photo-based Feelings and Emotions cards from SEAL (Social Emotion Aspects of Learning) very good. In fact, many of SEAL's resources are useful and a whole load can be found at: www.exploreyoursenses.co.uk/autism-toys/emotions-learning-understanding.html.

Feel Good Faces is a game for children with some understanding of questions and emotions already. Practise acting out emotions for others to guess, answering questions to boost awareness of what you are good at and doing silly tasks. The game needs an adult to support, guide and explain.

The popularity and motivation gleaned from Thomas the Tank Engine has led to a video and online game to help children with ASD understand emotions. Research has backed up the DVD as an effective tool: see www.thetransporters.com and www. hitentertainment.com/portal/us/games-thomas-emotions.asp.

Helping children learn ways to regulate emotions – through self-management and looking to others to help them

A useful book with lovely illustrations which provides a platform for talking about getting angry: Yolen, J. and Teague, M. (2013) *How Do Dinosaurs Say I'm Mad?* New York: The Blue Sky Press.

A card game that can help your child to learn different strategies to control their anger: Mad Dragon cards.

As we talked about in Chapters 1 and 8, you can make up your child's own calm box related to what works for them and make or buy individual resources for this box. You can also buy sets of Fidget Calming Kits from Amazon to get you started.

The Incredible 5-Point Scale is a resource to help children understand what they do and feel like with different emotions and different intensities of emotions. It also helps them to (with the support of an adult) think of appropriate things they can do by themselves or with the help of others to manage these feelings: Dunn Buron, K. and Curtis, M. (2012) *The Incredible 5-Point Scale: The Significantly Improved and Expanded Second Edition.* Shawnee Mission: AAPC Publishing. See www.5pointscale.com.

This is a book recommended by a friend. She found it beneficial to help frame our prompts and give lots of supports for emotional regulation. For some children it has also been a useful toolkit: Brukner, L. (2014) *The Kids' Guide to Staying Awesome and In Control: Simple Stuff to Help Children Regulate their Emotions and Senses.* London: Jessica Kingsley Publishers.

Events

The awareness of ASD is growing across the world and as such so is the service sector's response to the need to provide more positive experiences for families and people with ASD.

Across the UK there are autism-only screenings in different cinemas. Dimensions is an organisation that provides training and advice to help these occasions happen and so you can find out a lot of information from their website: www.dimensions-uk. org/families/autism-friendly-environments/autism-friendly-screenings.

Most cinemas also offer a free ticket for the carer of the child. You will need to show proof of their disability. In the UK you can attain a card from the Cinema Exhibitors Association (CEA) which you just show when you buy your tickets: www.ceacard.co.uk.

Most areas have a card that you show at your local attractions to get a free ticket for the carer. This card you can also use at busy queues at places like theme parks, aquariums and at the zoo. Do not be afraid to go to the front of the line and explain that you have a child on the autism spectrum and they will accommodate you. In the South East of England you can get a leisure card for children with special needs called the Compass Card (check your local area to see if they have an equivalent): www.compasscard. org.uk.

In the USA you can apply for a local state ID card. You can also apply for a Disability Identification card which you can use for identification purposes when applying for discounts: www. disabled-world.com. If you go to the contact tab and get in touch with them they can give you all the information you need.

For an overview of the benefits of engaging children with the natural environment and ideas for outdoor learning, see the Natural England Commissioned Report NECR116: 'Engaging children on the autistic spectrum with the natural environment: teacher insight study and evidence review.' First published 28 June 2013, available at http://publications.naturalengland.org.uk/publication/11085017.

For resources exploring benefits, places and stories about nature and autism, see autismandnature.org.uk/resources.

Airports will offer additional assistance for booking in and getting through security. Gatwick Airport has a family and disability security check which you can use. They can provide special access lanes and golf carts to take you straight to the boarding gate. On the Gatwick Airport website they have a section called 'Hidden Disability' which will give you all the information on how to plan your journey. The Heathrow Airport website also has an assistance section.

Evidence-based research

When seeking and deciding on approaches and interventions to support those on the spectrum you can be bombarded with information, promises and various small-scale research or case studies claiming success for all sorts of approaches. It can be intimidating and confusing. As each autistic person is an individual they will respond differently to different supports. There are places that can help you investigate the evidence base for interventions you may be interested in.

Research Autism is the only UK charity entirely focused on research into interventions for autism. Its website tells you about various interventions, and is easy to navigate in an alphabetised structure. It also provides ratings for the evidence available for each intervention, from very strong negative evidence, strong negative, negative, no evidence, mixed/insufficient evidence, positive, positive/strong evidence to very strong and positive: http://researchautism.net.

If you want to read more about the study we talked about in Chapter 1 (linked to what was called 'super-parenting' in the media), it's this one: Pickles, A., Le Couteur, A.,Leadbitter, K., Salomone, E., Cole-Fletcher, R., Tobin, H. *et al.* (2016) 'Parent-mediated social communication therapy for young children with autism (PACT): long-term follow-up of a randomised controlled trial.' *The Lancet 388*, 10059, 2501–2509. Available at www.thelancet. com/journals/lancet/article/PIIS0140-6736(16)31229-6/fulltext.

This is the study we talked about in Chapter 2: Cohen, S., Conduit, R., Lockley, S.W., Rajaratnam, S.M., Cornish, K.M. *et al.* (2014) 'The relationship between sleep and behaviour in autism spectrum disorder (ASD): a review.' *Journal of Neurodevelopmental Disorders 6*, 1, 44.

The study about habits which we talked about in Chapter 2 may provide you with more to think about regarding what it takes to form and change habits. However, be mindful that this is not a study on people with autism: Lally, P., Van Jaarsveld, C.H.M., Potts, H.W.W. and Wardle, J. (2009) 'How are habits formed: modelling habit formation in the real world.' *The European Journal of Social Pyschology 40*, 6, 998–1009.

To read more about the study we talked about in Chapter 3, please see Stewart, P.A., Hyman, S.L., Schmidt, B.L., Macklin, E.A., Reynolds, A., Johnson, C.R. *et al.* (2015) 'Dietary supplementation in children with autism spectrum disorders: common, insufficient, and excessive.' *Journal of the Academy of Nutrition and Dietetics 115*, 8, 1237–1248.

For the systemising theory discussed in Chapter 6: Baron-Cohen, S. (2009) 'Autism: the empathizing–systemizing theory.' *The Year in Cognitive Neuroscience: Annals of the New York Academy of Sciences 1156*, 68–80.

Explaining to others

This is a very personal choice for you and your family. Autistic adults have differing views on if or how to explain to others about their needs. There are some resources you may find useful if you are worried about what to say to your family or what to say to people when you are out and about. These resources can also be useful for young children or those unable to explain their needs to others if they do not have someone with them to advocate.

There is a useful card that you can give out, explaining that the person is on the spectrum with some facts about autism; it was developed in consultation with autistic people. It's available to buy from the National Autistic Society at www.autism.org.uk/Products/Core-NAS-publications/Autism-Cards.aspx.

MedicAlert is a charitable organisation providing bracelets, necklaces, sports bands and shoelace tags, which will have some core information and can link in with medical records to communicate your child's diagnosis and needs. Some of the jewellery has been designed in conjunction with Anna Kennedy – a mother of two children on the spectrum. It can become part of your safety plan in case your child wanders off. The organisation also provides support services and advice: www.medicalert.org.uk/about-us/about-us.

Finance

In the UK, there are sources of financial support that your child may be entitled to once diagnosed with a disability including ASD.

You can apply for Disability Living Allowance (DLA). This is not worked out on what you earn. Parents over the years have shared that they have used it to support additional toys, resources or clubs to attend. You can apply online at www.gov.uk/disability-living-allowance-children.

Dependent on your child's level of need (deemed middle or high from the DLA) you may or may not be entitled to Carer's Allowance. You can apply online at www.gov.uk/carers-allowance/how-to-claim.

If you are working and your child receives DLA, you are entitled to additional Child Tax Credits.

We will mention a charity within this finance section as so many parents have reported very positive experiences of being supported to fill in the DLA forms. However, this charity does so much more in giving information, connecting you with other families and inviting you to informal workshops. It is Contact: https://contact.org.uk.

Having a child on the spectrum may mean you use more utilities than most. Contact your local utility companies to see what they can do for your family. For example, Southern Water and Thames Water offer families a discount process and a capped process.

Flexibility and creativity

Cognitive flexibility is linked to cognitive processes known as executive functions, which includes controlling of attention, inhibition, working memory and flexibility. This then goes on to higher functions to not only have these processes available but also to use them in planning, reasoning and problem solving. We cover this in so many of our sections here in this chapter as you will be supporting flexibility in all aspects of day-to-day routines, social situations and communication. Many of your activities will also be incredibly creative.

You can teaching flexibility through visual supports, including timetables. Once your child can predict what is going to happen and is showing an understanding of the way you are sharing your routine through words, symbols, pictures or objects, you can use this same system to teach surprises, from positive to more neutral and then less desirable events/things. We have already suggested some websites for visuals; however, the visual supports section from the National Autistic Society has some additional ideas/ links to explore: www.autism.org.uk/about/strategies/visual-supports.aspx

A firm favourite with children and adults alike is Lego therapy. This uses an intrinsically rewarding activity and a clear system of rules and different roles of engineer, builder, supplier and director to work together. It gives opportunities to practise a range of social skills including compromise and problem solving. See LeGoff, D.B., Gomez de la Cuesta, G., Krauss, G.W. and Baron-Cohen, S. (2014) 'How to build social competence through LEGO-based clubs for children with autism and related conditions.' London: Jessica Kingsley Publishers.

The following book gives you a way to approach stories through chanting and scaffolding. Although often used with people with profound learning needs, it has been observed to bring laughter and creativity to story times for those developing their early language skills in nurseries and young people with autism: Park, P. (2004) *Interactive Storytelling: Developing Inclusive Stories for Children and Adults*. Bicester: Speechmark.

A useful book taking you through the set-up and running of Integrated Play Groups: Wolfberg P. (2003) (English Edition) *Peer Play and the Autism Spectrum: The Art of Guiding Children's Socialization and Imagination*. Shawnee Mission: Autism Asperger Publishing Company.

Frameworks

There are many frameworks that structure their approaches based on the best information known so far and are discussed and advocated during parent and education programmes alike. TEACCH is an approach that follows the core principles of teaching, using systems that are effective, expanding in terms of increasing others' knowledge, appreciating the unique profile of each individual and collaborating as well as treating the child in a holistic way. It strives to look at more than specific skills but includes the child in all aspects of community using structure and visual teaching. See http://teacch.com/about-us.

The National Autistic Society has produced its own framework, SPELL, which stands for Structure, Positive approaches and expectations, Empathy, Low arousal and Links. See www.autism. org.uk/spell.

SCERTS is a largely educational framework that has grown in popularity in recent years. We feel it is useful for families to consider as it looks to develop all aspects of social communication, emotional regulation and transactional support. See www.scerts.com.

Interior ideas

A good alternative to a night light is a Himalayan salt lamp (you can buy these online from Amazon and prices range from £10 to £20).

A memory foam mattress is useful to support sleep and those children seeking deep pressure. These can range in price. As long as it's a memory foam mattress and not a spring-based mattress you don't need to spend a fortune on it. A memory foam mattress is available from any local high street bed shop.

You can buy specially designed sleeping tents from a number of retailers. There are also some other alternative sleep solutions, including sleeping tents and supports available at www.safespaces. co.uk.

You can purchase any sort of tent for a play tent. You can go for a traditional camping one or a cool teepee, even a sheet over a few chairs. It's all about making a little safe space for your child to go in that blocks out a lot of other distracting elements of the home.

'One stop shops'

These are all charities or non-profit organisations that offer a breadth of information on ASD, explore supports for children, adults and their families and offer additional services themselves. Often these organisations also lead on research or trialling new ways of doing things. They all advocate for those on the spectrum in wider society, running campaigns to raise awareness and develop understanding of ASD.

UK: National Autistic Society: www.autism.org.uk.

Northern Ireland: services can be found on the National Autistic Society website: www.autism.org.uk/services/ni.aspx.

Ireland: https://autismireland.ie.

USA: Autism Society: www.autism-society.org.

New Zealand: Autism New Zealand Inc: www.autismnz.org.nz.

Australia: Autism Spectrum Australia: www.autismspectrum.org.au.

Parental journey

It may be useful for you to read about other parents' experience of receiving a diagnosis and leading family life with ASD. These journeys can be explored in books and, increasingly, blogs.

The following book gives an intimate view of family life with two sons on the spectrum. With no holding back on the challenges, the author takes you with her as she researches the disorder and tries out various therapies and interventions for both her boys. In the past she had written for *The Guardian* a column called 'Mind the gap' about her family experiences and she has featured on a number of occasions since. The book is: Moore, C. (2005) *George and Sam*. Harmondsworth: Penguin.

For a well-written book that describes the family's experiences with honesty and humour, try Stevens, C. (2008) *A Real Boy: How Autism Shattered Our Lives – and Made a Family from the Pieces*. London: Michael O'Mara Books Limited. It's sad at times yet is an inspirational read. Lynn is a mother of four and one son is autistic. She gives an account of her family's life with stories to promote understanding and give hope: http://ablogaboutraisingmyautisticson.com.

Day-to-day experiences with a hint of humour delivered in a factual manner and offering some practical ideas: www.theautismdaddy.com/search?updated-max=2017-01-01T11:56:00-05:00&max-results=7.

The recipe book by Gwyneth Paltrow which I mentioned in Chapter 3 is: Paltrow, G. and Turshen, J. (2013) *It's All Good*. London: Sphere.

Respite holidays

Respite can be invaluable to help you deal with the day-to-day challenges that can come in supporting your child with ASD. Talking to family and friends to explore what supports can be offered is a good start. You can also independently pay for services locally so do talk to the team around your child.

For those children with very complex and challenging needs you may be able to apply for respite services (day help such as outreach/play schemes/specialised child minders or overnight placements in specialised centres) from the government. You will need to contact your local authority and social services for an assessment to consider a care plan for your child and family.

You may be able to contact charities who will offer financial support and bursaries for holidays. The NHS website has a section 'Your guide to care and support' and this has a good list to start with. See www.nhs.uk/Conditions/social-care-and-support-guide/Pages/breaks-for-carers-respite-care.aspx#bursaries.

Home-Start is a charity that offers practical help through home visiting as well as emotional support to families with young children that need a little extra help for a range of reasons, including having a child diagnosed with ASD. See www.home-start.org.uk.

Support groups

Some parents find support from others experiencing something similar invaluable. There are discussion forums online run by all of the 'one stop shop' sites on ASD mentioned above. These sites will also tell you of local branches for parents that are set up. The previously mentioned charity, Contact, offers workshops, information sessions and parent support too. We would also encourage you to speak to the team involved with your child as there are many groups that are specific to your area that they will be able to recommend.

Understanding ASD

There are many different ways to develop your understanding of ASD. It can be from talking to others, reading a book, attending a parent information course or completing one online, watching videos or reading books explaining it from an autistic person's perspective, reading articles or blogs. We have come up with a range of these that you may want to take a few minutes to watch or in fact invest more time to attend or read in depth.

Books

The following is a mammoth book that explores ASD historically and challenges conventional thinking through this historical journey and indeed the author's change in his own thinking. It advocates for a greater understanding and acceptance for those with ASD with the opportunities to have full participation in society: Silberman, S. (2005) *Neurotribes: The Legacy of Autism and How to Think Smarter About People Who Think Differently*. Crows Nest, NSW: Allen & Unwin.

Another book we recommend is written from the perspective of a child with ASD by his mother. It is a hopeful book that is easy to read and really does help you to understand ASD. It starts with his strengths and even find positives in the challenges: Notbohm, E. (2012) *Ten Things Every Child With Autism Wishes You Knew*. Arlington, TX: Future Horizons Incorporated.

Based in the 'country of autism', the following book is written by a scientist who is autistic, resulting in a unique 'no nonsense' insight into the experiences of herself and others living in this 'country of autism', explaining her visual thought processes clearly and how these can significantly differ from others without ASD: Grandin, T. (1995) *Thinking in Pictures and Other Reports From My Life With Autism*. London: Bloomsbury.

Another book by Grandin provides an overview of her life and insight into how it feels to be labelled: Grandin, T. (first published in 1986, new edition 2005) *Emergence: Labeled Autistic. A True Story*. Grand Central Publishing.

The following is a useful article exploring the complexities of ASD and giving direction for resources and supports: Mitchell, D. (2017) 'What my son's autism has taught me.' *The*

Guardian. Available at www.theguardian.com/society/2017/jul/08/david-mitchell-son-autism-diagnosis-advice.

Books for siblings
There are some really great books out there for siblings and friends to understand ASD. Some of our favourites are:

Call, N. and Featherstone, S. (2013) *My Big Brother*. Featherstone Education. London: Bloomsbury.

Demonia, L. (2012). *Leah's Voice*. Houston, TX: Halo Publishing International.

Shally, C. (2009) *Since We're Friends*. New York: Sky Pony Press.

Robinson Peete, H. (2010) *My Brother Charlie*. London: Scholastic Press.

Bishop, B. (2002) *My Friend with Autism*. Arlington, TX: Future Horizons.

Videos
You can tell this was made a while back; however, it still has impact, combining the sensory experience with explaining ASD from people with ASD: *A is for Autism*, a film by Tim Webb (1992).

This National Autistic Society video clip (www.youtube.com/watch?v=Lr4_dOorquQ) takes you on a brief sensory experience through the eyes of a child with ASD. Can you make it to the end?

Courses
The team within the area you live will be able to direct you to any workshops or locally developed parent courses if the following are not available.

There are EarlyBird support programmes: the EarlyBird (for under-fives) and EarlyBird Plus (for four- to eight-year-olds). Both are comprehensive courses that will help you understand ASD, providing guidance on things to try to improve communication, interaction and behaviour. See www.autism.org.uk/earlybird.

Cygnet is a course for parents/carers of 7–18-year-olds, helping you understand how someone with ASD experiences the world and what drives behaviour, with practical advice and things to try. See www.barnardos.org.uk/cygnet/yk_cygnet-parents_carers_support_programme.htm.

Other

This article covers Ros Blackburn's view on ASD and has some useful suggestions: Blackburn, R. (2000) 'Within and without Autism.' *GAP (Good Autism Practice): Celebrating the First Ten Years of the Journal.* Published in partnership with The University of Birmingham Autism West Midlands and Autism Cymru.

You can find information all about Robyn Steward and her work in training and consultancy on her website: www.robynsteward.com.

This is a free book to help others understand the female experience of ASD: http://autisminpink.net. Go to the menu tab, scroll to book and you will be taken to a page where you can download Breaking the Silence online book.

We hope that some of the suggestions in this chapter will help direct you to useful resources and reading. You will never stop learning; sometimes this will be enlightening, frustrating and exhausting. It will get easier, often once a successful recipe of routine, structure and expectations has been worked out for your unique child and family. In fact, many parents have shared long periods of calm and happiness with autism at home. We wish you all the best in striving towards this.

INDEX